Praise for
The Quality of Effort

"This book will make you stop and think, and ask if we're doing what is best for our children. Mr. Marra has done a beautiful job preparing the coach, parent, and student-athlete for what's ahead."
>—Kieran Stack, 1989 & 1990 Irish National Champion, 3,000 meter Steeplechase

"The connection that I have always felt lies so strongly between sports and life is apparent throughout this book . . . it is a must read for anyone. I like the clear, concise way that nutrition, muscle physiology and training are presented—simple things that people are not aware of."
>—Lisa Toscano, Assistant Athletic Trainer; Instructor in the Department of Physical Education and Biology, Manhattan College

". . . Reggie Marra touches on all of the important aspects of coaching, parental concerns, and appropriate athletic perspectives. From Pop Warner to the professional ranks, this book is mandatory reading."
>—Harold Crocker, Head Football Coach, Iona College

". . . an excellent concept. . . . This is a needed and valuable contribution to our sport literature."
>—Rick McGuire, Ph.D., Head Unive

D1369783

". . . extremely insightful and informative . . . it is refreshing to read a book like this that covers such a wide scope of athletically-related moral issues and situations. I would recommend it to youths who are just beginning to compete as well as to adults who are parenting athletic youths or first entering a coaching career."
—Julio C. Diaz, Jr.,
Assistant Athletic Director,
Fordham University

"If you're interested in the development of human potential, *The Quality of Effort* provides excellent insight into the necessary knowledge, attitude, and skills."
—Michael McGrath, Dean of Students,
Iona College

"While everyone is obsessed with the 'All-American,' Reggie Marra cares about the everyday athlete. As I read *The Quality of Effort*, I had constant flashbacks to my high-school playing days. I know that if I had had this book back then, all of my athletic experiences would have been more productive and more enjoyable. This book will hit home for anyone who has ever competed in sports."
—Mike Breen, Sportscaster,
WFAN Radio, New York

". . . I really enjoyed [Reggie Marra's] convictions, his passion, and, of course, the *fact* that he is 100% correct."
—Craig R. Cirbus, Assistant to the Head
Football Coach, Penn State University

THE QUALITY OF EFFORT

10/22/92

Dear Lawrence,

Thanks very much for your interest in this book. I hope you find it to be of some value.

Best wishes,
Reggie Marra

THE
QUALITY
OF
EFFORT

Integrity in Sport
and Life for Student-Athletes,
Parents, and Coaches

REGGIE MARRA

FROM THE HEART PRESS
NEW YORK

Library of Congress Catalogue Card Number: 90-84335
ISBN: 0-9627828-0-7

Manufactured in the United States of America

10 9 8 7 6 5 4 3 2 1

The author gratefully acknowledges permission to reprint excerpts from the following:

"The Hero," by Kris Kristofferson. Copyright © 1990 by Jody Ray Publishing. All rights reserved/Used by permission.

The Road Less Traveled, by M. Scott Peck, M.D. Copyright © 1978 by M. Scott Peck, M.D. Reprinted by permission of Simon & Schuster, Inc.

Sports Health: The Complete Book of Athletic Injuries, by William Southmayd, M.D. and Marshall Hoffman. Copyright © 1981 by Quick Fox. Reprinted by permission of the Putnam Publishing Group.

Sports Illustrated, September 28, 1987. Copyright © 1987 by Time, Inc. SCORECARD—"Spiked." Edited by Steve Wulf. All Rights Reserved.

A World of Ideas, by Bill Moyers. Copyright © 1989 by Public Affairs Television, Inc. Reprinted by permission of the Bantam, Doubleday, Dell Publishing Group, Inc.

Thank you also to the people at Little, Brown and Company and at Sterling Lord Literistic, Inc. for their helpful responses to my inquiries.

This book is for
Bridget R. Marra and Reginald A. Marra, Sr.,
my parents,
who lived the quality of effort long before
I ever thought to attach a name to it.
And,
for Anne Marie and José Ramirez.

Contents

	Thanks	viii
	Foreword	xvii
	Preface	xix
ONE:	The Quality of Effort	1
TWO:	Becoming an Athlete	15
THREE:	How to Practice	25
FOUR:	Winning, Losing, and Competing— A Perspective	33
FIVE:	The Varying Natures of Success and Justice	41
SIX:	Athletics and Life: A Permanent, Positive Relationship	47
SEVEN:	Parenting the Student-Athlete	53
	NCAA, NAIA, NJCAA, NSCAA, NCCAA: Who They Are, and How to Find Out What You Should Know	65
EIGHT:	Coaching the Student-Athlete	75
NINE:	Drugs, Sex, and the Student-Athlete	81
TEN:	Cheating	89
ELEVEN:	The Student-Athlete and the Classroom	105
TWELVE:	The Quality of Effort—Hindsight	107
	Index	111

Thanks

THOUGH I HAD, as a youngster, played around with various sports, I began a serious relationship with basketball after my eleventh birthday. The earliest influence came from my cousin-"big brother," Don Marra, whom I watched as he consistently buried corner jump shots for Dobbs Ferry (N.Y.) High School. His willingness, during his high-school years, and despite our six-year age difference, to include me in everything from games of H-O-R-S-E to wiffleball, was both helpful and fun during my grade-school years. Thanks, Don.

Pete Griswold, who lived two houses away on Etville Avenue, over a period of several years, put up a series of backboards and rims just as quickly as some of our neighbors and the Department of Public Works could knock them down. When several of the basic nail-the-backboard-to-the-telephone pole arrangements proved to be too vulnerable to the tops of garbage trucks, Pete built and attached a hinged apparatus to a tree so we could raise the rim to about twelve or thirteen feet when it was not in use. Unfortunately, they chopped the tree down. Finally, he built a portable goal that we could wheel away and store in his driveway when we were done playing. They never figured that one out. Thanks, Pete.

When I began coaching in 1975, I had learned ninety-five percent of what I knew about basketball from Jerry Houston. He has influenced me as a teacher and a coach, and I'm happy to say that a solid friendship developed and has grown since our paths first crossed in 1970. I learned from his intensity, competitiveness, skill, and knowledge as a player and a coach, and from his sense of humor and class as a human being. His confidence, encouragement, and enthusiasm during some difficult times at Sacred Heart High School were, in fact, early lessons in the quality of effort. There are no legitimate substitutes for good teachers or good friends. I am fortunate to have found both in one man. Thanks, Jerry.

Thank you, also, to Brother Thomas J. Jensen, C.F.C., who, by his example, taught me that it's all right not to compromise certain values and truths, regardless of the wealth or title of those who desire or demand the compromise. He took the time to encourage a young coach back in 1979, and he reinforced his encouragement in writing two years later—not a word was wasted. From Power Memorial to Bergen Catholic, and everywhere in between, his students have over-achieved in the classroom, on the court, and on the field. Thanks, Tom.

Jim Lewer, Sr.'s influence was invaluable for many athletes in North Yonkers during the 1970s and 1980s. He taught them to work hard, to compete, to have fun, and to avoid making faces and whining when things didn't go their way. He is still competing today, in a different, more challenging arena, and his strength, spirit, and resilience remain sources of inspiration for all who know him. Thanks, Jim.

Thanks to Mike McGrath, teacher, coach, counselor, dean, and, across the board, the best educator I know personally, for providing me with job opportunities just as quickly as I can turn them down. His ability to assess both immediate and long-term situations accurately and to then make sound, timely decisions, has been a legitimate and appropriate reality check for me over the years. His caring and loyalty as a friend are even more valuable.

Thanks to Neal Murphy, Tony Giannelli, Joe Occhino, Dave Mytych, and Steve King, all of whom, as coaches, teachers, and good people, shared their knowledge, skill, and example with the young men in our program. Thanks, also, to the teachers, students, and staff at Sacred Heart High School for their encouragement, support, and friendship between 1968 and 1988.

Thanks to Mike Philp for years of friendship and for convincing me, against my better judgment, to run the Yonkers Marathon.

A special word of thanks goes out to Tom Rogers for his spiritual guidance-by-example. He and his family are constant reminders for me that love and the human spirit are ultimately more important and more powerful than money. It's not easy, but it's true.

Thanks to the CHSAA coaches, especially Mike Mincieli, Fred Opper, Bob DiNardo, Br. Louis Esposito and Brian Payne. They deserve thanks, and then some.

Paul Tepikian and I were good friends for about ten years during childhood and adolescence when the phrase "best friends" seemed to become appropriate. I'm happy to say that through many changes, the appropriateness has remained. From Yonkers to Carlinville to University City to Houston, every stride, every rooftop, every water balloon, and even every broken heart, has been made better by the friendship. Thanks, buddy. Here's to the next thirty years and beyond.

Thank you, from the bottom of my heart, to all of the strangers, acquaintances, and friends who lent their personal and professional integrity and credibility to my work while it was still a pile of typed pages: Mike Mincieli, Lisa Toscano, Craig Cirbus, Kieran Stack, Lou Carnesecca, Harold Crocker, George Sheehan, Lou Duesing, Mike Breen, Julio Diaz, Richard Lapchick, Kathy Solano, and Rick McGuire. Their kind endorsements and encouragement have been invaluable.

Thank you to Andrew Hoffer, who offered me expertise and expedience. In the process of delivering both, he provided care, enthusiasm, and affirmation, and he consistently told me that there's no such thing as a stupid question each time I asked one.

For her ability to create what I could only vaguely describe, and for her sense of humor, thanks to Donna Rocco, who provided the plunger of my dreams.

Thanks to Steve and Denise Georgian, Paul and Liz Tepikian, Tony and Elaine Manzolillo, Alice and Robert Stephens, and Bruce Tepikian, for their faith in me, and for putting their money where my heart and mouth are. I appreciate it more than the interest will ever say.

Finally, to the Three Strangers, Kris Kristofferson, Bob Knight, and John Gardner (1933–1982), thanks. Their work in their respective fields is straight from the heart and an ongoing inspiration to me.

Foreword

FROM THE FIRST TIME I met Reggie Marra, I knew he had a lot to give. It is the great good fortune of parents, student-athletes, coaches, and all who care about kids and sport that he has chosen to give us *The Quality of Effort*.

Having worked side by side with him, I have been witness to the living as well as the writing of this book. The "quality of effort" that he puts into his teaching, coaching, writing, and living demonstrates that these words are verbal expressions of real deeds done on behalf of the very audience for whom this book is written.

I only wish that you, the reader, could have been a student in his classroom, a player on his team, or a friend in his life. For then you would know from experience the quality of effort that gives his life its definition. I am glad that now at least you can hear his voice—a voice that speaks with great power to this listener, who knows that he means and lives all that he has written.

As a father of four student-athletes, I have found this book sensible, to the point, instructive, and brave. Imagine a writer who is not afraid to confront issues head-on with sound values, directness, and an unmistakable love of kids and sport— in that order! I do not have a doubt that all will benefit from his concise reflections on the philosophy of sport and the educational development of the human person.

We are treated to his story, which is enough like our own, to establish the identification that the stories of elite sports heroes make impossible. At the same time, this hero's story teaches us the lasting value of hope, hard work, and persistence in the building of a productive human life. This down-to-earth story presents the day-to-day realities and truths that our children need to be fed on since most of them will live their lives, not in the professional sports arena, but in the even more challenging world of family, career, and society.

It is truly refreshing to hear the good sense behind his critique of the individuals and organizations in the world of sport who often miss the point (instinctively, we knew it all along, whether at the Little League game or the NCAA meetings, but Reggie Marra comes right out and says it): kids are the most important part of sport—not parent egos, not winning traditions, and certainly not money. We know in our hearts that sport helps grow good kids. Reggie Marra *shows* how sport, in its proper perspective, combines with academics, values education, health, and family to do just that— grow good kids—and God knows the world has never needed more the good kids who grow into good adults.

Perhaps it is no accident that a book this honest, this right-minded, this unbiased, comes to us in a private printing. Those life players who reduce all things to profit and profiteering have seldom given us what we and our kids really need. Reggie Marra gives it to us in this rare book.

Tom Rogers
Husband, Father, Teacher
Tucson, Arizona
September 1990

Preface

THIS IS NOT a skill-specific book. The content, in and of itself, will not teach you how to kick a field goal, hit a home run, serve an ace, paddle a canoe, or perform any other athletic feat. Specific examples will pertain to basketball and running —these are the two areas with which I have the most experience. Yet, this is neither a basketball nor a running book. If I have done my job, and you do yours, the combination of my writing and your efforts will, I hope:

—Introduce you to and help you to understand what is meant by "the quality of effort," and how it affects you.

—Help you to become a better athlete—physically, mentally, and emotionally—regardless of your sport.

—Help you to learn how to practice and develop the sport-specific skills that you need.

—Put winning, losing, and competing in an appropriate perspective.

—Help you to understand the varying natures of success and justice—to see that our preconceived notions of what each should be often do not coincide with reality, and what we can do when they don't.

—Help you to see how athletics relates to the rest of your life, and how it can remain a permanent, positive part thereof.

—If you are a parent, make suggestions that are designed to help you do the least harm and the most good for the athleticism of your son or daughter; if you understand that his or her participation is for his or her own benefit and enjoyment, and not for your ego or lost youth, your chances for success are good.

—If you are a coach, give you some food for thought concerning why you coach and what you are trying to accomplish.

—Help you to understand, and make wise decisions concerning, the dangers of drugs and the experience of sex in your life.

—Help you to understand the diverse forms that cheating can take, and convince you to assume a state of mind that will reject cheating in sport and in life.

—Identify athletics as one component, among many others, of your growth as a balanced human being.

By design (and the recognized realities of my limitations), this book is not meant to be the last word on nutrition, practice techniques, parenting, coaching, drug abuse, sex, the NCAA, cheating, success, justice, or winning and losing. My intent is to provide a simple, diverse overview of the athletic experience—again, for parents and coaches as well as for the student-athletes. My own experiences as an athlete and a coach, along with the lessons I have learned from the ongoing lectures, clinics, and publications that my mentors make available, have enabled me to accomplish some worthwhile tasks. I genuinely hope that the ideas contained herein can help the reader toward some worthwhile accomplishments, small or large, of his or her own.

THE QUALITY OF EFFORT

*Would it bother you to know that
you can be just as good
as you really want to be?*

from "The Hero"
by KRIS KRISTOFFERSON

ONE
The Quality of Effort

ALL OF THE POLITICAL and religious leaders, entrepreneurs, professionals, entertainers, athletes, blue-collar workers, white-collar workers, the unemployed, the defendants, plaintiffs, victims and criminals in the world, whether they make the front page or the nightly news or not, are playing their own games. So are you; so am I. The games vary according to player eligibility, rules of conduct, and worth to society, but they are consistent in that success—winning the game—is highly favored over failure—losing the game.

Success looms as one of the most nebulous concepts with which we humans deal. Trite as it may sound, most of us see only title (power or fame) or fortune as the true symbol of success in our lives. The boundary line, the profit margin, the final score, the grand prize—all get in the way of too many otherwise successful people. The goals are not bad in and of themselves. We would all rather win than lose—that's healthy. It's when nothing else matters but the win or the profit margin that we start to have problems.

Nothing is more important than the quality of effort that goes into a particular endeavor. This quality of effort will usually determine whether or not the final goal is achieved at all, yet, it is often sadly neglected while the participants flail away, blindly focusing on nothing but the coveted prize.

Occasionally, extraordinary talent or a competitor's poorer quality of effort will allow an undeserving participant to achieve the final goal. Such achievement, despite its outward signs of "victory," is ultimately empty and ephemeral in the satisfaction it provides the victor. The right combination of genes or a competitor's default cannot replace the human

1

need to know that he or she deserves the award. This knowledge can only be realized as the result of a quality effort; victories attained without this knowledge may seem to satisfy, but it is a satisfaction founded in ignorance, not in effort, and is therefore only the appearance of satisfaction.

Without a genuine focus on the quality of effort, participants who fall short of their perceived final goal—be it a hostage release, an end to racism, a large profit, corporate salvation, or a national championship—will feel as though they have wasted their time—that they have failed—the prize is not theirs. *With* a genuine focus on the quality of effort, participants who fall short of their perceived final goal will be able to assess their participation and derive a very real sense of satisfaction and success from that quality of effort.

The historic 1984 women's Olympic Marathon did not end in failure for the silver medalist, Grete Waitz, because Joan Benoit Samuelson ran a great race. No one was a "loser" in that competition. Dr. Martin Luther King, Jr.'s life did not end in failure when he was assassinated in 1968. His heroic struggle against racism is perhaps one of the best examples of a successful effort whose final goal is yet to be achieved.

A genuine effort in any endeavor improves the quality of the participant. The improvement might be in a physical skill, a body of knowledge, a sharper intellect, or a better sense of the self and the rest of the world; if the effort is real, the improvement will be there. It might not always jump out and grab us by the throat; it might tap us gently on the shoulder or whisper in our ear. We must feel it—listen to it.

If the only reason we're shooting five hundred jump shots a day, studying for eight hours at a time, or working eighteen-hour days is to win the scoring title, win the scholarship, or win the promotion, there is a good chance that we'll fail. Complement these final goals with an enjoyment of shooting, studying, and working, and a desire to become a better shooter, student, or member of the work force, and there is virtually no way that we'll fail. The effort must count for something in our lives.

Though I had worked very hard at it since the seventh grade, I learned very little about basketball until my junior year in high school. My cousin, Don Marra's, soft corner jump shots for Dobbs Ferry High School in the mid-sixties aroused my interest, and the local boys' club gave me the opportunity to play in an organized league, but other than jumping off the correct foot for layups, and not crossing my feet on defense, I learned minimal fundamentals. I needed the fundamentals.

Fundamentals. Athletically, the seventh grade was a turning point for me. Of course, I didn't know what a turning point was then—I simply made a decision to do something. The fitness tests that tortured grade-schoolers consisted of side-straddles, squat thrusts, and sit-ups, among other exercises, and I finished somewhere in the middle of the pack in the two minute sit-up time slot. I think I did forty-four. Neither outstanding nor demoralizing, that total essentially proclaimed mediocrity, and that night it dawned on me that I could probably improve my performance on the eighth-grade test if I did sit-ups every night for the next year. Simple—if you want to improve at something that requires no talent, and only effort, make the effort.

One year later, having spent two or three minutes a night doing sit-ups, I did ninety-two in the two minute time slot. I felt pretty good about that.

The grade school that I attended didn't have a basketball program, so my first year of organized basketball put me in the local boys' club. My season high was sixteen points, and though I didn't know it at the time, it would be the highest point total that I would score in an organized game. My stellar performances in high school and college intramurals don't count. Too bad.

Eighth grade found me in the boys' club's next level, still a starter, but with a somewhat limited role. Ahead lay high school and freshman basketball—I couldn't wait—being part of a team, representing a school, practice every day. What more could a fourteen-year-old ask for? Talent.

During the spring of both eighth and ninth grades, my best friend, Paul Tepikian, and I ran in a number of quarter-mile, half-mile, and mile races. Much to our surprise, we consistently won, placed, or showed—this with never having run more than a mile in preparation, and usually attired in cutoff jeans, white tee shirts, and high-white canvas Converse All-Stars. Brother Basilian, one of the Christian Brothers at the high school, tried to convince me to run cross-country and track. All I wanted at the time, however, was the big orange ball. Suffice it to say that Brother Basilian was better at selecting the right sport for the right student than I was back then.

I spent the summer working on my left hand and on foul shooting. I didn't know any specific drills, but I shot over and over and over again, and I approached the freshman tryouts limited only by my lack of talent and experience. Some twenty-odd boys who had played several years of CYO ball in grade school were cut from the team. So was I. The coach had spoken one sentence to me in three days of practice: "Don't be afraid to shoot." Then he told me what he really meant by leaving my name off the list that he posted in the locker room—my first experience with being cut.

The boys' club had an interclub team for fourteen-year-olds who were not playing in high school. I made the team and spent most of my time on the bench. I still enjoyed practice and the games, but the high-school team practiced almost every day; we practiced once a week. I wanted more involvement. I eventually got it too, but not quite in the form for which I had hoped.

Over the course of my sophomore year, I variously operated the scoreboard, kept the book, and kept stats as manager of the junior varsity basketball team. In a very shallow way, I was a member of the team, but it was not what I ultimately wanted. The boys' club program didn't have a league for fifteen-year-olds, so my playing was relegated to the park and high-school intramurals.

The biggest thrill during this 1969–70 school year was spending subway fare and four dollars for a blue seat and a nosebleed next to the pigeons at Madison Square Garden. Down below, Reed, DeBusschere, Bradley, Frazier, Barnett, Russell, Jackson and the rest enchanted us while we chanted for them. We loved them all, but every schoolboy wanted to be like Clyde—and wound up speaking like Marv Albert. I would have gladly traded my number 10 jersey, my "*Yes! And it counts!*" imitation, and my blue seat for a spot on the high-school team that year.

Junior year brought a coaching change to the high school and introduced me to one of the most influential people in my life—an accurate description, even as I write this. I hadn't really known the varsity coach during my first two years at the school, so his leaving had little effect on me. Rumors about the new coach were popular during September, and time gradually proved most of them to be fact. He had played at St. John's University, a senior cocaptain during Joe Lapchick's final year—1964–65. He had made the winning free throws in the 1964 Holiday Festival and the 1965 National Invitation Tournament, and he held the single game scoring record at LaSalle Academy on 2nd Street in Manhattan—69 points—a record that still stands today.

Jerry Houston was stronger, quicker, and more talented than, and almost as tall as, every player who would try out for his team in 1970. He could jump, he could shoot, he could pass, and he saw everything on the court; he was scary on defense. If that weren't enough, at just under 6'2" he played harder than anyone I had ever seen. Better yet, he was talented *and* he understood the game. Many talented individuals never quite figure out how or why they are successful athletes. Mr. Houston could teach the game that he played so well.

For the first time now, my classmates would be competing for spots on the team against a group of seniors who already had a year or two of varsity experience. Some would be cut for the first time in their lives—some would make the team. I wound up at the scorer's table again. I attended most of the practices as a junior and was exposed, along with the players, to Houston's knowledge, intensity, and competitiveness. Some of the players, especially a senior or two, resented him. I thought he was great, but, then, I wasn't running my butt off on the court.

Toward the end of the season, just after a halftime talk that appropriately addressed the reasons for a thirteen-point deficit, one of the seniors, on his way back to the court, spoke a sentence that had a strong impact on me. He had been overweight early in the season, and his playing time had been limited until he made the effort to shed some pounds. As we walked from the locker room that afternoon, he spoke to one of his teammates: "I hate that man." That man was the coach.

I may have been naïve, but to say that I was surprised would be an understatement. I was also annoyed. Here was the best coach any of these guys is likely to meet in a lifetime, and this genius hates him. That afternoon I vowed to myself that I would play on the varsity as a senior. Even without this motivation I would have wanted to play, but I became obsessed with the idea that Jerry Houston deserved players who were willing to appreciate what he had to offer. Unfortunately, I was 5'6" and 125 pounds, quick, a good jumper, but with marginal basketball skills at best. And, if my general skills were marginal, my shooting ability was off the page entirely. I figured that my two main advantages were that I'd be in better shape than anyone else, and that I knew my limitations. Looking back, I was probably right on both counts.

That night I began a regimen that would take me through the end of the school year, into the summer, and right up to the opening day of tryouts in October. Had I known then what I've learned since, the specifics of the regimen might have been different; the overall purpose would, however, remain the same. I worked every day to improve both my athletic ability and my basketball skills. The workout included the daily sit-ups, which I had continued since seventh grade, a complementary dose of push-ups, regular full- and half-court games in the park, foul shooting and weak hand drills when the games were over, four nights a week of barbell jump squats and ball-handling drills in the basement, and an occasional one or two mile run. I know now that I should have been shooting five hundred jump shots a day, but that wisdom escaped my sixteen-year-old mind.

The tryouts began in October with some twenty-eight juniors and seniors seeking spots on the team. Only three players were returning from the previous year's senior-dominated squad, so a large number of current seniors who hadn't played joined the juniors who were attempting to move up from the junior varsity.

My approach to the game made me a mixed blessing to other players. I never played at half speed or "dogged" it in the drills or scrimmages. Never. I knew that I couldn't afford to. I also appreciated how much more fun it is to defend someone who doesn't have the ball yet, so I played defense—hard. All the time. I denied the ball. I helped. I boxed out. If there was a loose ball that I had a chance at, I got it.

On the other hand, my most highly developed offensive skill was passing, so I could be valuable to have as a teammate, especially if you liked to score—I'd give you the ball when you were open. I'd rather pass than shoot—the odds for my success were better that way.

During the week of tryouts, I watched twenty-eight become

twenty-three, then twenty, then fifteen, and finally, on that Friday in October, a Friday that included a 3:30 practice, the final cuts, a 6:30 appointment with the dentist, and a senior class mixer, I watched the fifteen become twelve.

Fifteen of us were still actively involved when we entered the full court scrimmage in the last half hour, and while some of the players present took their spots for granted, we all knew that three of us wouldn't be back on Saturday morning.

Coach Houston spoke to the players who came out as he substituted during the scrimmage, and during two of those brief, face-to-face conversations, a couple of good friends received their bad news. One of the players who was still up would be the thirteenth man on the twelve-man roster. I continued to work my butt off, conscious of how close I was to what I wanted, and I tried to avoid looking nervously in the coach's direction. My goal was to make the team—not to avoid getting cut.

Where I didn't look, and what my goals were, aside, I recognized all too well the next name that he called.

"Reggie." I ran over and looked up at the man who had the authority to say, "Stay" or "Go." My mind raced almost as fast as my heart beat while I stood there dripping with sweat in my Dobbs Ferry sweat shirt with the sleeves cut off, the faded and tattered kelly green Sacred Heart gym shorts with the gold trim, the knee pads, the two pairs of thick, sweaty socks, and the classic, high-white, canvas Converse All-Stars.

"I want to thank you for coming out for the team," he said. "But I'm going to have to cut you. You have a great attitude, and you've done everything that we've asked, but we already have four guards." I felt the lump in my throat pushing upwards in an attempt to squeeze out the salty water that was filling my eyes, but I swallowed hard, and not a drop escaped. "I'd like you to consider being our manager again this year. You helped us out a whole lot as a junior—don't make up your mind right now—give it some thought. We'll be in at

9:00 tomorrow morning—you're welcome to get dressed and run with the team if you like."

I'm not sure what I said, if anything, there on the sideline or downstairs in the locker room after practice when some of the players tried their best to offer consolation. The bus ride home as darkness fell, a change of clothes, the drive to the dentist, and then to the blur of the senior mixer, all blended into a night best forgotten—a sequence of events that would end only when I decided whether or not to manage the team. I showed up at 8:30 the following morning. The decision to stay with the team has since opened some worthwhile doors in my life.

The alumni game on Thanksgiving eve in 1971 marked my official low point and the beginning of my recovery from having been cut. One of my classmates, who had repeated a grade in elementary school, was declared ineligible for interscholastic competition because of his age, and a distant ray of hope that, perhaps, his spot would become mine appeared on the horizon. When that ray never brightened, I sat through the pregame meeting, the warm-up, and the game itself, watching the players in their home whites with a deep sense of envy and disappointment.

Coach Houston must have recognized my mood, and after the game, with most of the players already gone, we were walking up the back stairway that joins the locker room and the gym, when he asked me, "Is everything all right?"

I didn't look up and replied, "Yeah."

He persisted. "Are you sure?"

I looked at him this time and managed to force out a fairly convincing, "Yeah, everything's okay." I could have cried right then and there.

"If there's ever anything I can help you with, don't hesitate to ask," he concluded. He meant it too. I was lucky enough to understand that there is but one way you become a member of a team: you earn it; you don't campaign for it. I still believe that today. I was also either lucky or naïve enough to persist in my belief that I could make a college team somewhere—freshman, JV, any level or affiliation—I didn't care. The conditioning and practice regimen continued in preparation for October 15, 1972, wherever that date would find me.

As luck would have it, by the spring of 1972, my college choices were narrowed down to the State University of New York at Albany and St. John's University. I would board at the state school, but commute to St. John's; Albany had a respected Division III program, and St. John's was obviously Division I, pre-Big East, but with a marginal junior varsity team in what would be the first year of freshman eligibility. The upstate school provided a quality education with very reasonable tuition, room, and board; the Queens school provided a quality education, and they offered me an unbeatable financial aid package. Give me a roll of quarters and aim me toward the Throgs Neck Bridge.

Frank Alagia and "Beaver" Smith would be freshman starters for St. John's in 1972. Ron McGugins also earned a varsity spot as a frosh, and five other recruits held down positions on the junior varsity. Some forty-odd off-the-street hopefuls would compete for the other seven JV spots.

A thirty-pound weight jacket had imposed itself on my workouts over the summer, and the aisles in the blue and red level seats at Alumni Hall beckoned during the six-week period between the start of classes and October 15. A typical day, after classes, included from one to two and a half hours of half court games on the main court and then twenty round trips up and down the arena's stairways, resplendent in thirty-pound attire. Severe leg cramps after one ill-advised, postworkout dip in the pool precluded swimming as a regular part of the routine.

Take a group of marginal high-school basketball players who have just met, divide them into groups of five, sprinkle them lightly with sweat, and feed them to a traditionally powerful Division I basketball team, and what do you get? Junior varsity tryouts. One three-quarter court pass that led to a layup, and one layup of my own later, my name failed to appear on the sheet of yellow paper that was posted outside the men's locker room after the second day. The scalpel felt much the same as it had during my ninth grade operation.

I decided to give myself one more chance to represent a school on the basketball court. Sophomore year would be it. If I couldn't make a JV team as a sophomore, I was bright enough to realize that "walking on" St. John's varsity as a junior with no previous interscholastic or intercollegiate game experience on my resumé would probably be too much of a long shot—even for me. Such insight!

The half court and weight jacket workouts continued in Alumni Hall. At home, jump squats and ball-handling drills in the basement complemented the full court runs and thousands of free throws and jump shots in the park. I learned that shooting practice, from a success-failure ratio point of view, is probably a lot more fun if you're a pretty good shooter at the outset. But I did it anyway. My shooting got better, but it wasn't completely well—only the October operation, once again in the face of the scalpel, would tell for sure.

My summer job with the local parks department enabled me to spend two weeks with Coach Houston at a basketball day camp in the local middle schools. I led the younger campers through their drills and all the while listened to the coach's every word and watched his every step. He continued to teach me simply because he knew that I wanted to learn.

October 15, 1973 rolled around quickly, and I stepped onto the court in the best shape of my life. The bad news is that even this final operation fell short—the scalpel found its now familiar victim quickly and easily. The good news is that despite all the cuts, the patient didn't die. He got better.

I continued to play, to run, to listen, and to watch. I

watched Lou Carnesecca in his first year back at St. John's, and I watched Jerry Houston up at the high school. The practices were as interesting as the games—teaching is an art— whether it's American Literature or defensive rotation.

The parks department job enabled me to spend another two weeks coaching basketball over the summer, and junior year in college dawned with the unique prospect of my not trying out for a basketball team. Once again, the fall and spring semesters rolled past, and the summer brought an unexpected, but welcome, opportunity.

The last slice of pizza had just disappeared from the table at Maggi's Restaurant when Coach Houston asked me if I'd be interested in coaching the freshman team at the high school. After checking my fourth-year course load at St. John's, I accepted the position. I worked for two years on the freshman level, moved to the junior varsity for three years, and I coached my first varsity season in 1980–81. Jerry Houston spent that season as an assistant with Tom Penders at Fordham University, and then moved on to the business world. He's still The Coach, however, and a good friend, and every year there is a group of young cagers in Rockland County who are the better for his being in the neighborhood.

In 1987–88, our team won the Division IV Championship in the New York City Catholic High Schools Athletic Association, and finished second in the New York State Catholic Schools playoffs on the class C level. Unfortunately, we lost five seniors, including three starters and a sixth man, to academic problems after the first round of the city playoffs. This loss left us with only four players—juniors Don Kelly and Shawn Bullock, and senior starters, Sam Byrd and Mike Ostrander. Freshman "K.J." Koch and sophomores Mike Mueller, Kenny Dronzek, and Charlie Baker joined us from the junior varsity for the remainder of the playoffs. To the credit of these eight young men, when they were finally eliminated from the New York City Catholic School Playoffs, it was at the hands of the eventual class B City Champs, Nazareth High School. The margin of victory was seven points.

There you have it. The good news is that there are thousands of similar stories worldwide. Maybe millions. Real athletes work hard, compete, improve, strive toward their potentials, and derive a sense of joy, accomplishment, and pride from their efforts. Real people do the same with their lives. The levels of success and justice in their stories vary, but success and justice seldom live up to our preconceived notions of what each should be.

There are quite a few legitimate, often quiet heroes who make six and seven digit annual salaries in sport. Good for them. There are a thousand times that many who make somewhere between nothing and several thousand dollars a year teaching young athletes well. Better for them. Finally, there are those, who at some time in their lives, took the extra hundred jump shots, ran the extra mile, swam the extra laps, or lifted, swung, paddled, stretched, jumped, kicked, threw, served, skated, or whatever—proceeded beyond what was merely required, and never made an excuse for the result. Best for them.

TWO
Becoming an Athlete

EVERYONE WHO PARTICIPATES in sport should be physically fit. Of course, sport-specific needs vary: you can "get away with" less fitness in baseball than you can in basketball; golfers don't need the aerobic capacity of marathoners; swimmers and weight lifters have different aerobic and anaerobic needs. The comparisons and contrasts are endless—and pointless.

The point is that an appropriate balance of aerobic and anaerobic fitness will not hurt you and will help you. Even athletes such as golfers, whose sport relies almost exclusively on skill rather than on conditioning, can benefit from being in shape. Ask a serious golfer about the need for stamina during a seventy-two hole tournament.

As a high school basketball prospect, I knew that my skills, especially my shooting ability, were below par. In addition to practicing those skills, I had to be in better shape than anyone else—just to be competitive. Some players were going to beat me because they were more talented; I was determined that no one would ever beat me with less or equal talent and better conditioning.

As athletes get tired, especially if their conditioning is subpar, their performance deteriorates, and their minds convince them to take it easy. They have not conditioned themselves to compete with some discomfort. As this happens, they think that they are "having a bad quarter," or inning, or set, or round, or what have you. Think what they might, the well-conditioned athlete, talented or not, has an edge late in a contest.

Ideally, or so I see the argument logically develop, what

15

happens when a superb talent decides to develop fitness as well as natural skill? That athlete is difficult to defeat, physically, mentally, or emotionally. I want him or her on my team. Pick your favorite sport and study the people who are considered among the best: you will undoubtedly find talented athletes who have conditioned themselves to excel.

What follows here is a brief overview of some basic concepts of athletic training. Conditioning and injury prevention and treatment are essential areas of knowledge for student-athletes, parents, and coaches alike. Two of the earliest sources of such information, which I benefited from as a coach and as an athlete, and which are still available today, are: *The Sportsmedicine Book* by Gabe Mirkin, M.D., and Marshall Hoffman and *Sports Health: The Complete Book of Athletic Injuries* by William Southmayd, M.D., and Marshall Hoffman. These two volumes have helped me through Achilles tendinitis, separated shoulders, torn hamstrings and various other minor injuries. Of course, no book is a substitute for professional care, but these two are worthwhile resources for the lay reader who is active in, or concerned with sport.

Training is generally characterized as being either aerobic or anaerobic. Aerobic training develops the ability of the body to provide oxygen to the muscles during exercise—it conditions the heart and the other muscle groups for prolonged activity. It is training *with oxygen.* Marathoners, cross-country cyclists, and distance swimmers are examples of aerobically-fit athletes.

Anaerobic training conditions the body for exercise *without oxygen*— the pace or intensity of the workout does not allow the heart to pump enough blood to replenish the oxygen that is needed by the muscle groups used. Sprinters and weight lifters are examples of anaerobically-fit athletes—intense demands are put on specific muscle groups during a 100 yard dash or a dead lift, during which the muscles' oxygen supply is not sufficiently replenished. Where the marathoner has conditioned his or her body to perform well over a period of several hours, the sprinter has prepared for a few seconds of all-out effort.

Obviously, sports vary as to their requirements for aerobic and anaerobic fitness. Some require much more of one than of the other, some require a balance of the two, and some don't really require performance near either the aerobic or the anaerobic threshold. While these requirements vary from sport to sport, Mirkin and Hoffman, in *The Sportsmedicine Book*, point out that training for virtually any contest does require that the muscles be conditioned in varying degrees for coordination, speed, and strength (pp. 28–30).

Coordination is the process during which the brain, the senses (primarily, but not exclusively, sight and touch), and the nerves and muscles work together to perform a series of specific movements. In most cases the eyes send images to the brain, where they are interpreted, and the brain sends signals through the nerves in order to contract or relax the appropriate muscles. The process takes a fraction of a second —whether it involves a baseball player swinging at a ninety mile per hour fastball or a golfer tapping in a ten-inch putt. Practice—repeating the movement correctly, again and again, familiarizes the body with the movement (this familiarity is sometimes called muscle memory), and improves coordination. The athlete must master the correct movement —swinging the bat, kicking the ball, clearing the hurdle— slowly at first, with no mechanical mistakes. Once the movement can be performed slowly and correctly, the athlete can begin to work on speed.

Speed allows the athlete to perform a specific movement or series of movements faster, and can be a distinct advantage in almost any sport. Muscles are composed of both fast twitch and slow twitch fibers. Fast twitch fibers provide for muscular speed and strength. Slow twitch fibers provide for endurance. To be fast in competition, you must develop your fast twitch fibers—train for speed in practice.

The ratio of fast to slow twitch fibers is determined genetically at conception and varies from person to person—outstanding sprinters have a higher percentage of fast twitch fibers; outstanding endurance athletes have a higher percentage of slow twitch fibers. Regardless of your ratio, prolonged, paced aerobic training will develop your slow twitch fibers; quick, strong, anaerobic training will develop your fast twitch fibers.

An example: A friend of mine played high-school basketball and could dunk—an accomplishment that requires development of the fast twitch fibers. In his mid-twenties he began running, and eventually became a 2:30 marathoner. At the age of thirty-eight, still a runner, after thousands of aerobic miles, he can barely touch the rim (he is six feet tall). His slow twitch fibers have consistently developed, but since he no longer plays or practices basketball, his fast twitch fibers have not kept pace. Superbly conditioned basketball players will balance their slow and fast twitch development in order to provide for both the endurance that enables them to run up and down the court for thirty-two, forty, or forty-eight minutes, and the strength and speed that enable them to jump, sprint, move laterally, and stop quickly.

Speed work, be it for a golf swing, a runner's stride, or a football lineman's footwork, must be done, but only after the particular movement can be performed slowly and correctly. Practice the wrong movement quickly and diligently, and you quickly become very good at the wrong movement. A more detailed look at this potential problem follows in the chapter "How to Practice."

Strength conditioning makes the muscles stronger and is accomplished by working the muscles against resistance. Free weights, Universal, Nautilus and Cybex machines are examples of popular resistance equipment. A baseball player's swinging a weighted bat—actually performing the hitting motion against resistance—is a simple, sport-specific strength training technique. Strength conditioning isolates one or more muscle groups and works them against progressively stronger resistance.

Strength will only increase as the resistance is increased; increasing the number of repetitions done will build stamina, but will have little effect on strength. An example of this strength vs. stamina development follows: a friend and I both work out regularly with weights. I am 5'6" and 135 pounds and use light to medium range weights (50% to 75% of my maximum) with 12 to 15 repetitions per set and no more than 30 seconds (usually less) rest between sets. I am more interested in increasing stamina than the size or strength of my muscles.

My friend is 5'10" and 190 pounds—much more heavily muscled than I am. He starts with medium range weights and approaches and attempts to surpass his maximum as his workout progresses. As he increases the weight, he decreases the number of repetitions per set, and he rests as long as is necessary between sets. His maximum bench press is some 150 pounds greater than mine—he is much *stronger*—yet, I can do 25–30 more push-ups than he can before failure (failure is the point at which the muscles fail—you can physically do no more). My weight training builds stamina; his builds strength. Mine is more aerobic in nature; his is anaerobic. You must know what your goals are—strength, coordination, stamina, or some combination thereof—in order to train properly.

The final, and arguably most important, component of any fitness program is *flexibility*. Stretching helps to prepare the muscles and connective tissue for exercise and helps with recovery afterwards. Exercise injures muscles. Southmayd and Hoffman, in *Sports Health*, call this ordinary breakdown of muscle tissue due to exercise "micro-injuries." They explain, "When the muscles heal, they heal slightly shorter. It is the same as the healing of a scar. The scar tissue draws the wound together" (p. 56).

Exercise shortens the muscles. Stretching, done correctly, lengthens them, and it feels good in the process. For a thorough, sport by sport guide to proper stretching technique, see Bob and Jean Anderson's book, *Stretching*.

To a basic understanding of these four factors, *coordination, speed, strength,* and *flexibility,* you must add a familiarity with *training* and *overtraining, hard* and *easy days,* and *background* and *peak period training.* Remember, the body can be overworked, and even if it is not, peak performance may never be achieved if the timing is not right. Mirkin and Hoffman, in *The Sportsmedicine Book,* present a detailed, yet straightforward and easily understood explanation of these very important aspects of training. A brief summary of the essential points follows here:

—*Training and Overtraining:* The body can be overworked. An increase in the workload or intensity of a workout, or the implementation of a new training method should be monitored carefully. Overtraining can result in poor performance and injury.

—*Hard and Easy Days:* The muscles must be allowed to heal after intense work. Recovery does not necessarily mean complete rest (although when it is called for, it should be heeded), but rather, a less intense workout.

—*Background and Peak Period Training:* Background training gradually improves strength, endurance, and skill over a period of time. Peak period training involves working less, with adjustments in intensity, as competition approaches (pp. 30–37).

Whether or not you are a talented individual in your sport, it makes sense for you to be a well-conditioned athlete. If your skill level is low to average, being fit will give you an advantage—make you more competitive. If you have above-average talent, or if you are the very best in your school, town, or state, being fit will add a new dimension to your performance. Forget the opposition—see how good *you* can be.

If this sounds appealing, sit down with your coach or some knowledgable and experienced athlete in your sport. Figure out what it is that you are trying to become, and develop a program for yourself. Don't be shy. Any coach worth his or her title would rather work harder because you ask for help than because you don't.

For further reading on the training concepts that are introduced in this chapter, again, the following three books are an excellent place to start:

Anderson, Bob and Jean. *Stretching.* Bolinas: Shelter Publications, 1980.

Mirkin, Gabe, M.D., and Marshall Hoffman. *The Sportsmedicine Book.* Boston: Little, Brown and Company, 1978.

Southmayd, William, M.D., and Marshall Hoffman. *Sports Health: The Complete Book of Athletic Injuries.* New York: Quick Fox, 1981. (Currently handled by Perigree Books in New York.)

NUTRITION AND THE ATHLETE

No variation of aerobic or anaerobic training, slow or fast twitch fiber development, background or peak period training, or hard and easy days will benefit the individual who does not eat well. Literally hundreds of special diets have come and gone (a few have come and stayed), all the while claiming to aid athletic performance.

Some of these diets have had their specific benefits for particular athletes, but the majority of competitors today, if they are interested in nutrition and performance, would benefit most from information on a regular, balanced diet that includes the four food groups. This basic information is available from any doctor, nurse, or nutritionist; it can be found in virtually any bookstore or library; and it is published in brochure form by the National Dairy Council and other similar local organizations.

The four food groups are:

1. The *milk group*, which includes milk, cheese, yogurt, and other dairy products.
2. The *meat group*, which includes beef, veal, pork, lamb, fish, poultry, eggs, peanut butter, and other foods.
3. The *fruit/vegetable group*, which includes all fruits and vegetables, especially those that are sources of vitamins A and C.
4. The *grain group*, which includes whole grains, grain products such as certain breads, cereals, pasta, and rice.

In its simplest form, according to the National Dairy Council, the four-food group approach to nutrition provides for the following daily menu for teens and adults:

—Four servings (two for adults) from the *milk group*. (e.g., One serving = one cup of milk.)
—Two servings from the *meat group*. (e.g., One serving = two ounces of beef, poultry, or fish, or two eggs.)
—Four servings from the *fruit/vegetable group*. (e.g., One serving = a common portion of fruit, such as a banana, an apple, or four ounces of cooked vegetables.)
—Four servings from the *grain group*. (e.g., One serving = one slice of enriched bread, or one cup of ready-to-eat cereal, or 1/2 cup of cooked cereal, pasta, or grits.)

This plan provides for the recommended daily allowance (RDA) for many of the body's nutrients, and sufficient calories for a "normal" day's activities—approximately 1,500.

Athletes, who burn more calories than the average person, require additional caloric intake. This should be provided by eating additional servings of the four food groups, with the fruit and vegetable and grain groups being the preferred sources for this extra fuel. The meat and dairy products are higher in fat and cholesterol, and do not replace muscle glycogen, but again, a *balanced* diet is the key. Some additional guidelines, suggested by the National Dairy Council, are worth keeping in mind:

—Avoid skipping meals.
—Your eating habits should preclude any sudden, large weight gain or loss.
—Complex carbohydrates such as pasta, bread, and cereal are the most efficient fuel for athletic muscles to burn. Note, however, that carbohydrates *alone* do not provide for all nutritional needs. Stay with the four groups.
—Drink water, or some appropriate thirst quencher, before, during, and after competition, when such replenishment is possible.
—Avoid "unnatural" activities in order to meet certain weight restrictions. Not eating or "drying out" can lead to dehydration and will diminish performance and health.
—Read, ask questions, and be responsible for your own good health. A good place to start is Nancy Clark's chapter, "Nutrition" (pp. 392–423), in the previously-mentioned *Sports Health.* Also see *Nancy Clark's Sports Nutrition Guidebook* (Champaign, Illinois: Leisure Press, 1990).

Remember, all of the training and talent in the world won't get you anywhere if you neglect the nutritional needs of your body. Eat well.

THREE
How to Practice

UNFORTUNATELY, SOME OF YOU will be able to participate in a given sport up to a level of performance that satisfies you without ever coming close to your potential. Essentially, you will do the minimum that is required by your coach to get by —to make the team, to get playing time, or to start. Some of you will start because of your God-given talent, with virtually no effort at all. After four years of high school or college, you will be older, maybe a little bit more knowledgable, and maybe a little bit bigger and stronger. Your skill level, however, will be nowhere near its potential. I would like to suggest an alternative approach to your sport.

I will describe the approach shortly, but you can learn it by watching some of your less talented teammates or opponents, and often, you will see a talented, elite athlete using it also. When it is combined with an appropriate conditioning program, I believe it is the best approach to improving performance—whether you are ranked number one in your sport in the state, or you are not sure if you are going to make the team.

The simple, proven method to improve at virtually anything, from brushing your teeth, driving a car, tying your shoes, or operating a computer keyboard, to hitting a baseball, shooting a jump shot, hitting a backhand, or paddling a kayak, is mechanically correct, progressively quicker repetition.

Mechanically Correct: Be sure you can perform the movement correctly before you repeat it; practice the wrong shooting motion, golf swing, or running stride diligently, and you will become very good at the wrong motion, swing, or stride.

It is usually much easier to learn something correctly from the beginning than it is to relearn it after doing it incorrectly over a period of time.

Progressively Quicker: It is easier to both learn and assess the accuracy of any movement when the movement is done slowly at first. After you have captured the movement accurately and slowly, you can gradually develop the appropriate speed.

Repetition: Perform the movement over and over and over again in order to develop muscle memory. Once you have developed both accuracy and speed, you must continue to practice, to repeat.

Watch some friends or family members brush their teeth or drive their cars. Many, if not all, of us have sacrificed accuracy for speed in these two familiar activities. This does not mean that we all exceed the speed limit when we drive or miss our teeth when we brush, but, rather, that our mechanics have become sloppy—we don't signal, come to full stops, or use acceleration lanes properly when we drive, and we don't clean our teeth thoroughly when we brush. We are so concerned with what we are going to do next—get home, get to work, the beach, or the store—that our technique suffers. The same will happen with sports if we fail to practice. We must concentrate on what we are doing, and not on what we will do next.

There are literally hundreds of different movements that we could use to launch a basketball toward the rim, move a golf ball off a tee, or move our legs alternately in order to run. Not all of these movements are particularly effective. Thus, good coaches everywhere teach virtually the same mechanics for the jump shot, the golf swing, or the runner's stride. Sure, we all have our own little idiosyncrasies and pet peeves, but the essentials vary very little.

What follows here is an example and description of one approach to learning and practicing the jump shot. While this example is sport-specific for basketball, the approach can be applied to virtually any sports skill once the specifics of the skill have been identified.

TEACHING THE JUMP SHOT: ACCURACY, SPEED, AND GAME CONDITIONS

When we teach a young athlete how to shoot a jump shot, we use demonstration and imitation in order to convey the fundamentals of stance, grip, arm position and motion, release, and follow-through. We demonstrate the correct movements, and the student-athlete imitates as best he or she can. We make corrections and adjustments until the form is acceptable. In most cases, the student-athlete has been heaving the ball toward the basket for a year or more already.

Occasionally, a coach will come upon an athlete whose mechanics are, to the human eye, all wrong, but whose results are excellent. This is a judgment call, which, though it is never easy, does get easier with experience. No one, whether he or she is shooting 33% or 93% from the free throw line, wants to change from what feels comfortable. We have an obligation to help the 33% shooter with mechanics. While every case should be viewed individually, the 93% shooter should probably be left mechanically intact.

Depending on the specific player's skill level, we may or may not use a ball when we first teach the motion, release, and follow-through. Once we do use a ball, we may "shoot" it at a wall or toward another player rather than at the basket at first; in this way the student-athlete can concentrate on the mechanics without any anxiety over whether the ball goes in or not. Once we've reached the point of comfort with the motion, the ball and the basket, we begin the process of repeating close-in shots.

When Brian Winters played with the Milwaukee Bucks, he was considered one of the best, if not the best, shooting guards in the National Basketball Association. When he combined his shooting lecture with the following semicircle drill at summer camp, the result was perhaps the ideal warm-up for any basketball player before beginning shooting practice, and an excellent learning drill for a beginner.

The drill can be started on either side of the basket; for this example, we will start on the right side. Begin one step back from the rim, with the sidelines in front of and behind you, and the baseline to your right. Make this short "corner" shot, and keep your arms extended in follow-through until the ball hits the floor (shot #1). Retrieve the ball, move one step to your left, and shoot the bank shot (use the backboard). Again, exaggerate the follow-through in order to make sure it is correct. Continue moving to your left around the rim. Shots #1 through #7 should be equally distant from the rim, as should the shots in each subsequent semicircle (as in #8– #14 and #15– #23). The practicing player should continue the drill until he or she is out of shooting range—the point at which the shooter is unable to comfortably reach the basket. Note that as the semicircles get farther from the basket, the number of shots taken in each will increase.

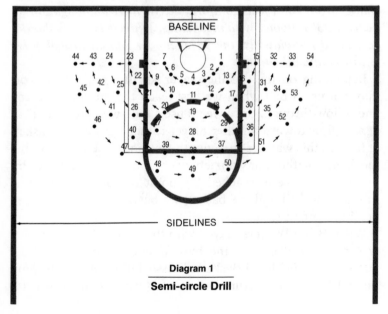

Diagram 1

Semi-circle Drill

A summary of the general rules for this drill follows:

—Don't move back more than one step after each semicircle.
—Don't move on to the next spot until you make the shot in your current position.
—Keep your follow-through extended until the ball hits the floor. The follow-through tends to deteriorate due to fatigue late in a contest (this is true in any sport). By exaggerating it during practice, the athlete stands a better chance of maintaining it once he or she grows tired.
—Practice *shooting the ball.* Don't simply try to finish the drill. Experience has shown that concentration, as much as natural talent, leads to success with this drill.

Many high school players with whom I have worked hurry through the drill in order to finish. They should, in fact, take their time and concentrate on their form and on finding their range. If all that concerns an athlete at practice is finishing, the practice will, more often than not, be a waste of time.

Once the proper form and movement have been developed and are still being practiced, we move on to developing speed and to simulating game conditions. No one gets to shoot in increasingly larger semicircles in a game, and while we cannot reproduce actual game conditions—the noise, the officials, and the reality that the clock and the score "really matter"—we can simulate certain important factors:

—Shoot on the move, at full (game) speed.
—Set a measurable goal in order to create pressure—keep score.
—Compete (in this case, shoot) when you are tired.
—If a teammate is available, shoot against defensive pressure.

The drills that exist that will meet these criteria are limited in number only by the imaginations and the needs of the athletes and coaches. One of the best drills of this kind is Rick Pitino's $+6 -6$ (or $+4 -4$). This drill can be used to practice shooting from any spot on the floor, or any individual move, such as a jab step and drive, or a baseline drop step. It can be used if you plan to practice for five minutes (probably not a great idea), or five hours. All that you need is a ball, a hoop, and some discipline. With imagination, the principles that follow here can be applied to creating similar drills for virtually any sport.

For this example, we will practice a seventeen foot jump shot from the right side foul line extended, cutting to the ball from the baseline:

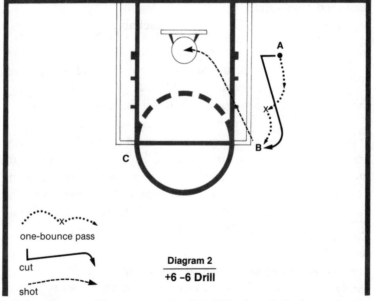

one-bounce pass

cut

shot

Diagram 2
+6 –6 Drill

The player will start at point A, ball in hand, facing point B, from which he will take the shot. The player will toss the ball underhanded, with backspin, toward point B so that it will bounce up waist to chest high. The player will *run* behind the ball, catch it on the first bounce, square to the basket, and shoot the jump shot. The player should use either a two foot jump stop or a plant and pivot move in order to square to the basket. Finally, the player will follow the shot, rebound the ball whether it goes in or not, quickly dribble the ball to point A, and, again, toss the ball to point B for the shot.

The scoring system works as follows, and should be adjusted for the skill level of the practicing player. Start at 0 and add 1 (+1) for every successful shot; subtract 2 (−2) for every unsuccessful shot (younger players might benefit from using −1 for the misses at the outset). Continue the drill until the score reaches either +6 or −6, or whatever the target game is (+4 −4 is easier; +8 −8 is much more difficult), at which point the player goes to the foul line for some predetermined task—make three in a row, or five in a row, or whatever is both challenging and reachable for the particular player.

Once the foul line goal has been attained, move to another spot on the floor, and begin the drill again. If you reached −6 from point A, it is best not to return immediately to that spot —move to another spot. Remember, the drill does not rely on the use of sixes—use what works for you.

It is essential that the drill be run at game speed, and that the shot or move being practiced is identical each time it is taken or made. For our example above, in diagram # 2, it would be incorrect for the player to toss the ball from point C and cut across the foul line to point B in order to shoot. Cutting left to right across the lane involves different footwork than cutting right to left up from the baseline. These are two different shots, and they should be practiced separately.

Again, the variations possible with such a drill are limited only by the needs and imagination of the player or coach. With an understanding of a sport and a relentless desire to improve, effective drills are relatively easy to come by.

* * *

While the above drills were described for individual practice, it should be clear that practice can be enhanced by the presence of an opponent, a coach, or a teammate. Mistakes in technique should be detected and corrected immediately before they become habit. Not all of us have the luxury of someone who is willing and able (knowledgable) to help us practice, but be aware that it can be very helpful.

Finally, the use of film or videotape enables the athlete to see himself or herself as he or she performs. Most of us are very surprised when we first see ourselves—when we don't look like Larry Bird, Edwin Moses, or Martina Navratilova, it's a blow to our egos. It also may be one of the single most helpful learning aids. If you have no access to film or tape, wait until no one else is home or in the locker room, and practice your form in front of a mirror. This is not an ideal situation, but it enables you to both see and feel your form simultaneously.

In summary, you must both want to improve, and be willing to work at it. Then you must learn the correct technique and repeat it, becoming progressively quicker, when quickness is appropriate, as you work.

FOUR
Winning, Losing, and Competing —A Perspective

MANY PEOPLE PARTICIPATE in sports for purely recreational or health reasons rather than for the competition. They enjoy the game or activity, so they play it or do it; whether they win or lose is irrelevent, as long as they take part. While I would hope that all athletes, competitive or not, enjoy what they do, this chapter has the competitive athlete in mind—especially the competitive athlete who might be losing sight of, or who has yet to see, what sport is all about.

Ask twenty different athletes—CYO, high school, college, professional, or whatever—what their goals are prior to a contest, and the answers will vary. Some will say, "To win." Others will say, "To play hard," or "To do my best." Few, if any, will say, "To get by," although some will do just that.

I try to convince athletes to believe in and to act upon the following: *Personal excellence, the individual's absolute best, is the ultimate goal; performance judged relative to others is limited by the performance of others.*

This philosophy says two simple things about opponents:

—Don't be happy with your performance *simply because you beat your opponent.*
—Don't make beating your opponent *the only result that will make you happy.*

It says one thing about you: *Be happy with your performance when you have done your best with the variables over which you have control.* If you are preparing for a marathon, you can control your choice of race, your diet, and the nature and distance of your workouts during the months before the race; you cannot control the twenty mile per hour head wind or the poor traffic control along the course on race day. Whatever your sport, learn to recognize those variables over which you do have control.

The examples below can help you to better understand this philosophy and to see more clearly the relationships that exist among winning, losing, and competing.

"THE POORLY-PLAYED WIN"

Our basketball team was playing against an opponent that had never beaten us. This particular season, we had three wins and two losses in our division, and they had no wins and five losses when we met. At the end of the third quarter, we led 49 to 36. Our players played the fourth quarter expecting to win; their players played as if they were trying to win. We won 60 to 58, though we did not deserve it. If the game had lasted a minute longer, it is likely that we would have lost. I am not saying that I wanted our team to lose—I didn't. But winning this particular game taught our players nothing worthwhile. Some of them saw their lack of effort and respect rewarded with a win and were happy. Some of them knew that they had been lucky to win. One or two of them knew that they did not deserve it. All of them heard the truth from me afterwards.

We had no great players, and we were a marginally talented team in a competitive league. Our opponent, and this is meant with the utmost respect, had less talent and athletic ability than we did, but had a much higher quality of effort. We had no business feeling happy or satisfied because we beat our opponent. Relieved, maybe, but not satisfied.

Or, an elite quarter-miler, against the best competition in

the world, comes out of the final turn with a five yard lead, and feeling strong. Believing that he has the race won, he lets up as he approaches the finish line and beats the second place finisher by mere inches, missing a world record by one tenth of a second. He beat his opponents. Should he be satisfied? Would you be?

"THE WELL-PLAYED LOSS"

In 1979, our junior varsity basketball team was down 80 to 60 at the end of the third quarter against a superior opponent that we had never beaten. Their players were bigger, quicker, and more talented than we were, but we left our hearts and souls on that court and outscored them 34 to 20 in the final period. We pressed, we stole the ball, we made our free throws, *we scored 94 points—40 points above our game average*—and the scoreboard said that we lost the game. On a relative basis we did lose—they scored six more points than we did. In an absolute sense, I believe that our players played up to, and possibly beyond, their collective potential that day. I'm not sure that that's losing.

Sure, it goes down as a loss in the league standings, but we put forth an excellent effort and were beaten by a superior team. I want our players to recognize such an effort, and to learn to appreciate it, regardless of the final score.

Let's go back now to that second place finisher in the quarter mile—the runner who almost won the race because the winner let up at the end. Our second place sprinter went out quickly and finished well—he ran an excellent race and reduced his personal record for the quarter by .62 of a second. But he didn't win. Is he a loser? Do you see the point? If I measure my success on the tennis court by comparing careers with Chris Evert, my success in the 110 meter hurdles on competition with Roger Kingdom, and my success as a quarterback based on Joe Montana's accomplishments, I'll be in big trouble. The entire problem will be with my head, however, and not necessarily with my performance. *Whether the competition is better or worse, if I assess my failure or success relative to that competition, I'm in for trouble. My potential within the event is my only competition.*

There is nothing wrong with using a superior opponent to *help motivate* us to excel. The problem exists if the opponent is our *only* source of motivation. We have to love the event, the contest itself. The truly great ones love practice too, because they understand that true mastery is not a level to be attained, but, rather, a path to be followed. In the May 1987 issue of *Esquire*, George Leonard, in "Playing for Keeps—The Art of Mastery in Sport and Life," wrote, "What is mastery? At the heart of it, mastery is staying on the path." Dizzy Dean put it rather well years earlier when he said, "When you stop getting better, you stop being good."

When I was cut from the junior varsity basketball team in college during my sophomore year, I was disappointed, but I walked away satisfied that the combination of my limited talent, size, and experience had produced that result. I did not feel that "if only I had worked at it," maybe I could have made it. The countless hours that I spent playing, practicing skills, lifting weights, and running had helped me to improve as a basketball player and as an athlete. I had given my best effort and had fallen short relative to the qualifications of the other players and the requirements for the caliber of play at that level.

Did knowing this make my immediate disappointment any less severe? No. But it enabled me to take the disappointment with no regrets—no "if only" phrases applied. I had addressed the variables that were within my control as best I could. My size and the size and ability of the competition were not my focus. I understood them and I forgot about them because I could not affect them.

Pay attention and devote your time and effort to what you can affect. Learn what is beyond your control, understand it, and forget it. Compete to win, but love competing—you must enjoy the event.

"IF YOU ARE TRYING OUT THIS YEAR"

If you are trying out for a team this year, what will you do if you:

—Make the team, earn a starting spot, and everything goes well?

—Make the team, don't start, but get a decent amount of playing time?

—Make the team, but rarely, if ever, play in the games?

—Get cut from the team?

Regardless of which of the above possibilities you expect will happen, use your imagination and try to envision your probable reaction to each of them. Really try to feel what it would be like to start, or to play sometimes, or play rarely, or get cut. What will *you* do?

Your reaction to each of the four possibilities should be the same (unless getting cut convinces you to give up sports entirely). Whether you start, get cut, or wind up somewhere in between, you should continue to work hard at your sport—develop your skill level and your athletic ability. If you make the team and stop trying to improve, you are selling both your teammates and yourself short. If you get cut and stop trying to improve, the sport is probably not all that important to you, and that's okay—as long as you're sure that you won't regret stopping some years (or months or weeks) later.

It all goes back to the basic philosophy—compete against

yourself and the contest—if you do this honestly, you'll do your best in terms of your opponents too.

I believe that this applies to all levels of sport, from the basic elementary school and instructional leagues through the professional ranks. In reality, however, there is one major philosophical difference that must be recognized between professional sports and all others. Grade-school, youth club, high-school, and college sports are all educational, recreational, and social in nature (at least they start out that way). While it can be argued that some high-school and college sports have virtually turned into businesses, this is a flaw in, rather than the intent of, the system.

Professional sport, on the other hand, is big business by nature. A player in the National Basketball Association stated that "there are no moral victories" in the seven game championship series. Simply getting to the final round does not satisfy the players—winning the title is the only satisfier. Here is a group of men, arguably the best in the world at what they do, and paid exceptionally well to do it. Because of their backgrounds in sport, their talent, and their salaries, they are expected to know their job and to execute it with a high degree of competence. Playing basketball is their job, and winning the title is the ultimate goal within their industry.

Athletes, parents, and coaches must recognize the difference between what goes on in Madison Square Garden and what should go on in the local high school gymnasium, on the Little League field or at the grade school fun-run. Not only are the rules of the games different, but the reasons for staging the games—for the games' very existence—vary by necessity.

The youth and adolescent games exist as educational activities. Some community pride and the desire for recreation and social interaction also encourage the events, but education is the foundation. The professional games exist as profit-motivated entertainment—business. Competitive pride and the joy of competition also encourage these events, but business is the foundation.

Some may argue that education is itself a business. This is true, but on most levels, it is far from profit-motivated. Its business nature enables it to exist from day to day. So, let's demand a lot from our young people—fitness, discipline, respect, sportsmanship, and a high quality of effort, in addition to their academic pursuits. Let's not make them entrepreneurs before their time.

FIVE
The Varying Natures of Success and Justice

IF YOU CAN UNDERSTAND and embrace the following sugges-
tion, perhaps the triumphs and disasters of your life, both in
and out of athletics, will be much easier to celebrate, tolerate,
or mourn: *Success and justice, though present in our lives in
varying degrees, will not always live up to our preconceived
notions of what each should be.*

How many times have we heard or said the words, "It's just
not fair," or "There's no justice in the world?" It may have
been after an athletic event when the other team won, or
after a minor accident, or a terrible tragedy, or a disappointment in our personal or professional lives. It may even have
been after someone, whom we deem as undeserving, got
good news—a promotion, a spot on a team, a raise, an en-
gagement ring, a scholarship, a great job, or a winning lotto
ticket—you name it.

We perceive many events and situations as being fair or
unfair, and successful or unsuccessful. That we do not *all*
perceive the same events and situations in the same way is
the focus of this chapter.

When high school *A* shows up at our basketball tournament, and from the head coach to the youngest fan behaves
like a band of boors—screaming profanity, abusing opponents and officials, pointing fingers on the court, and starting
fights—we feel that it is "unfair" and that there is "no justice"
when they win the championship and one of their players is
voted the most valuable player. They, however, have been
practicing since early November, just as we have, and despite

their behavior (which is a disgrace and should be confronted), they view their championship as both fair and successful. They didn't win because of their boorish behavior—in fact, they were clearly the most talented team in the tournament—but we feel that winners, and people in general, should behave better.

Joey B. is a brilliant high-school senior who does minimal studying. His SAT scores and his grade point average earn him a full scholarship to a good college. Mike T. studies two hours every night for four years and compiles a 78 average, which is at or near his academic potential, and he can't even get financial aid based on need—his parents have excellent incomes. Mike views the irony of his hard work and Joey's scholarship as being unfair. Joey, a nice enough individual, views Mike as a good friend, but has no problem with the correlation between his natural gifts and his scholarship. He earned the scholarship honestly, by doing the required work well and by passing tests. He views himself, and he is viewed by others, to be a success. He sees his scholarship as a just reward for the successful student that he is.

Our fictional family makes $35,000 each year. We work hard, shop carefully, and try to save what we can. Our good friends have a combined gross income of $250,000 a year. We all play lotto. They win $4.5 million. We congratulate them, but we know that there is no justice in the world—*it's not fair* —we needed the money more than they did. They, on the other hand, believe that they deserved a chance to win as much as anyone else (they're correct), and they will come up with at least as many uses for the money as we would have.

You can come up with your own examples. Some involve our "opponents," some involve people whom we know and who are "on our side," and some involve strangers whom we observe or about whom we hear. Regardless of the specifics, each of us judges the fairness or success of an event according to our preconceived notion of what it should be.

* * *

Webster's New World Dictionary, among several definitions for justice, gives us, "the quality of being righteous; impartiality; fairness; reward or penalty deserved." The same source defines success as "a favorable or satisfactory outcome or result," and successful as "coming about, taking place, or turning out to be as was hoped for or planned."

Most of us, whether we are consciously goal-setters or not, have definite goals that we would like to attain. The goals may be general—I plan to own a house near a body of water —or specific—within five years I will build a three bedroom A-frame on an acre of lake-front property on Lake Champlain; the house will have two fireplaces, etc., etc., etc.

Whether our goals are specifically stated or generally acknowledged, some of us will strive for what we want, taking risks and making sacrifices along the way, and some of us will simply wander toward what we'd like, waiting for, rather than creating, opportunities, and hoping that everything will work itself out.

Take the two young athletes who plan to try out for the high-school freshman basketball team. Alex would like to be on the team, so he plays basketball at the park whenever he knows his friends will be there and he's not working—he's trying to save some money so he can buy a car when he turns sixteen. Sammy, on the other hand, not only wants to make the team, but he wants to start. He practices at the park every day after school for two hours, and for longer periods on weekends. His practice schedule allows him virtually no time for television on weeknights: practice—dinner—homework— bed. He'd like to make some money, but he wants to make the team, so rather than do a marginal job at both, he takes a chance and sacrifices the money in order to give the basketball his best effort. This requires some courage.

Who do you think will be more disappointed if cut, or more satisfied if he makes the team? The more concrete our goals are, and the more serious our efforts are to attain them, the stronger our feelings of disappointment or satisfaction will be. We appreciate more what we've worked hard to get.

Two concepts, opportunity cost and serendipity, are related to our goals and affect our perceptions of success and justice. All of us learn about opportunity cost somewhere along the line. Maybe it's in a classroom—Economics or Consumer Education tells us that for every choice we make, we give something else up; maybe it's in the candy store—at seven years of age, we choose between the candy bar and the soda; maybe it's in our hearts—we leave behind the gorgeous dream date in order to be with someone, who, though not perfect, cares about us, is willing to share the good times and the bad, and whom we love.

Opportunity cost is that which is given up when a decision is made. Buy the candy bar, and in addition to the money, it costs you the soda. Date Kris, and it costs you a date with Al. Practice your sport diligently in high school, and it may cost you some money-making, parties, and television, among other things along the way. Don't practice diligently, and you may never know the full extent of what you gave up along the way.

Serendipity, according to *Webster's*, is "an apparent aptitude for making accidental, fortunate discoveries." M. Scott Peck, in *The Road Less Traveled*, provides another similar *Webster's* definition: "the gift of finding valuable or agreeable things not sought for." Dr. Peck goes on to say that:

> . . . one of the reasons we fail to take full advantage of grace is that we are not fully aware of its presence—that is, we don't find valuable things not sought for, because we fail to appreciate the value of the gift when it is given us. In other words, serendipitous events occur to all of us, but frequently we fail to recognize their serendipitous nature; we consider such events quite unremarkable, and consequently we fail to take full advantage of them. (pp. 257–58)

What should we do when we give our first love, middle distance running, everything that we have, and we find that our only real excellence is on the golf course? What if our goal is a Division I football scholarship, but we're offered "only" a full, four-year academic scholarship to an excellent university that has a Division III football program? How should we react when good things that we haven't pursued (or even considered) come our way?

The answer to this last question will play a major role in determining the extent to which we believe that success and justice exist in our lives. Not everyone gets to be a professional, or even a college or high-school athlete, or a movie star, or a recording artist, or a governor, or even to be happily married. When we have the courage to shoot for our ultimate dream with a high quality of effort along the way, and we fall short, we really do need something to catch us. For many, the love and support of family and friends are steps in the right direction. The safest net, however, is within ourselves—a balanced view of the world—and the ability to recognize, appreciate, and embrace serendipitious events and people can be a strong component of this balanced view.

The world owes us nothing, and sometimes we don't get what we really want. On the other hand, some very worthwhile, though unexpected, things come our way from time to time; we need only to recognize them and accept the good that they bring.

We have to come to terms with God's having created only one Michael Jordan, one Don Mattingly, one Wayne Gretsky, one Edwin Moses, and one Jackie Joyner-Kersee. Not all of us will realize our dreams of professional sports, entertainment, political, or entrepreneurial careers, but some of us will—and that's great, as long as we take our talents to the limit, and we accept and embrace the unexpected good that comes our way. Sometimes the only difference between the "successful" and the "unsuccessful" individual is the ability to see the forest despite the trees, and to hear, and then open the door when opportunity knocks. You'll be surprised how much more just life can become when you both see and hear clearly.

SIX

Athletics and Life: A Permanent, Positive Relationship

A RUDE AWAKENING awaited me at my first high-school alumni basketball game. None of my classmates was yet twenty years of age, but several friends, who had been good athletes in high school, arrived with fifteen or twenty additional pounds and what looked like fifteen or twenty additional years on their faces and torsos.

Even more disturbing was my experience at the alumni games that followed my first few years of teaching. Some of my former students returned, and they looked ten years older than most of the teachers who were present.

My focus here is not how these people looked—their appearance merely evidenced a more significant situation. In the space of one year, they had gone from being young, healthy student-athletes to old, overweight college students and members of the work force. They were still young chronologically, but, in terms of physical condition, they had aged beyond some people who were twenty or thirty years their seniors. I'm not suggesting that we need a world full of body builders and triathletes, but, rather, that we need some minimal levels of fitness and health.

It is true that as you progress through high school, on to college or work, and starting a family, each added responsibility saps a little more of that "free time" that you enjoy while you are young. When you get to the point, however, that your personal and professional schedules do not permit you to care for your physical well-being, it may be time to stop and reassess your priorities.

Of course, you can't neglect your studies, your spouse, your children, or your job in order to spend two hours a day, seven days a week in the gym, the pool, or on the track. You can, however, find the time—in fact, you will *make* the time —if your health is important to you. Some of us need one-half hour a day, three days a week; others want an hour a day for five or six, or seven days—you may need or want more or less. *You* decide.

Will you feel selfish "taking time for yourself?" Consider this instead: Will you feel selfish if you don't take the time, and your health fails you and you become a burden to the very people for whom you feel responsible? This is a worst case scenario. I am suggesting that you keep athletics in your life for two basic reasons:

—You enjoy sports.
—It's good for you—physically, emotionally, and mentally.

In the movie, *Rocky*, Adrian and Rocky spend their first date bribing the maintenance man at the skating rink for some ice time on Thanksgiving night. During their few minutes on the ice, they share some views on their bodies and their brains.

Rocky tells Adrian that his father told him that he'd better learn to use his body because his brains wouldn't get him anywhere. Adrian laughs and says that her mother gave her the opposite advice—she'd better learn to use her brain, because she didn't have much of a body.

The scene at the rink was both funny and poignant—each character shared a somewhat awkward self-perception with the other. The scene also portrayed a very real problem that many of us have today—perceived specialization. We're either smart or dumb, plumbers or politicians, athletes or scholars, black or white. Rarely do we get to be human beings who happen to have chosen certain careers or vocations, who enjoy sports and reading, and, who, for the sake of an example, have a knack for carpentry, but no clue when it comes to car repair.

Our society needs to group people—classify them—they're easier to figure out and sort that way. We group by profession, color, income, religion, sex, appearance, and other arbitrary characteristics. If you're a lawyer, we know what *that* means; or if you're Catholic; or if you're short; or if you're black, or white, etc., etc., etc., we know what that means too.

While you are in school, you may be a "jock" or a "brain." If you're lucky (and brave) maybe you're both. No matter what you are right now, or what you've been, the categories don't really matter except in people's minds, and while that can affect their perception of you, it does not affect *you*— who and what you really are. So, why not strike a balance? Why not develop athletically, as well as intellectually, emotionally, socially, professionally, and spiritually, as you grow chronologically older?

Twenty-five years ago, anyone who ran three or five or fifteen miles through the streets was considered an eccentric at best —at worst, someone to stay away from. For all practical purposes, the noun "aerobics" did not exist, and virtually no one, other than dancers, danced to music to keep in shape. Nautilus didn't exist at all, triathlons were unheard-of, and other than organized high-school and college sports and certain elite areas of competition, few athletic endeavors included women.

Today, whether you are a male or a female, if you want to compete, or simply stay fit, your options are many. Run, cycle, jog, swim, ski, skate, dance, lift, paddle, row, hit the heavy bag, play team sports, or do whatever you want, and no one will look twice. Wear a hot pink sweat shirt and bright green tights, clamp a headphone set on your head, and run around the neighborhood—you'll fit right in. Be traditional— gray cotton sweats and high-white Converse All-Stars; be state of the art—shorts or tights and singlet with $100.00-plus footwear; be whatever you like, but be good to yourself. Try different workouts, and choose the one(s) that you enjoy.

In the first chapter, we introduced the concept that the quality of effort—the integrity of what we put into a particular endeavor—is ultimately the most important factor in sport. We've now taken both that quality of effort and sport one step further, and applied them to the rest of our lives. How hard are you willing to work for your education, your loved ones, your livelihood, or your health? The discipline that you bring to the playing field, the court, or the other arenas is appropriate for the rest of your life. In fact, coached and played with integrity, sport can be one of the best preparations for the successes and failures, joys and frustrations, and solitary tasks and group efforts that we encounter in our everyday lives.

Ideally, through sport, we learn to enjoy victory without gloating, to suffer defeat with dignity, and to play according to an agreed-upon set of rules. We will continue to enjoy certain victories and to suffer certain defeats throughout our personal and professional lives. The lessons in sport, though important when experienced, are somewhat less significant and less painful than are our experiences with family, career, love, illness, and death, yet these former lessons can help us develop the intellectual, emotional, and physical tools that we need to cope with our latter experiences.

Both individual and team sports have worthwhile, though, at times, very different, values to offer. The trust, camaraderie, loyalty, and basic interpersonal skills that we need in the workplace, with our families, and with friends are definitely previewed in a healthy team sport environment. On the other hand, for those of us who must tackle more solitary tasks, or who must overcome personal dilemmas, there is perhaps no better preparation than the training required by the runner, swimmer, boxer, wrestler, cyclist, or other athlete, whose event, by nature, relies on the individual, rather than on a team effort.

Although we often do not recognize it while we are competing, no intramural, interscholastic, intercollegiate, international, or professional sports victory or defeat is as important or as meaningful as the triumphs we enjoy and the setbacks we suffer from day to day with our families and friends concerning our physical, emotional, mental, and spiritual wellbeing. So, make athletics a permanent part of your life. Enjoy it; learn from it; help others to do the same. Understand what winning, losing, and competing are all about, come to terms with the natures of success and justice in *your* life, and see how much more success and justice exist when you know what to look for.

SEVEN
Parenting the Student-Athlete

PERHAPS THE MOST FRIGHTENING, frustrating, discouraging, and unnecessary experience that a student-athlete can have is to be pushed, badgered, harangued, glared at, and embarrassed by a well-intentioned, ignorant parent who believes that all of his or her words and actions are forms of support and encouragement. *Ignorant* is the key word here, because most parents who pay enough attention to their children to attend their athletic contests really do what they do wrong out of ignorance, rather than out of jealousy, meanness, or vindictiveness.

This chapter should be the most difficult for some parents to read because it specifically addresses the most common, but least often admitted, shortcomings that caring parents display with regard to their athletic children. If you feel your blood pressure beginning to rise or your defenses getting ready as you read now, please trust what you've read so far and continue. The purpose here is not to accuse or insult, but to create awareness and offer support.

The situations that follow here are fictional. They undoubtedly have been influenced by what I have seen and heard over the years. The people described and the names used are fictitious, and any similarity to any real person is unintended and should not be inferred.

Some of the examples are extreme; some are commonplace. All of them can be negative experiences for young student-athletes, be they eight or eighteen years of age. The basic premise here is that sport should be both fun and beneficial (promoting health and social skills, developing sports skills, and dealing with victory and defeat) for the participants. Sport should not be a source of verbal competition among the parents of the participants; nor should it be an attempt by the parents to recapture their lost youth through the efforts and the triumphs of their sons and daughters. When your child loses, he or she needs to hear and feel your support— not your excuses, be they to the child or to observers. When your child wins, he or she still needs your support, and maybe some of your wisdom to temper the victory—not to minimize or downplay—but to keep it in a proper perspective.

We will proceed, despite the dangers of assuming, with the assumption that all of the parents who create problems for their athletic children do so inadvertently or carelessly because they care very much for their sons and daughters, and they feel good when their offspring perform admirably. Parents who deliberately demean, embarrass, or humiliate their children out of hate, jealousy, or meanness, are beyond the scope of this book.

"MISSING THE BIG PICTURE"

Martin starts at guard on the freshman basketball team. He is an average athlete, a below-average shooter, and a good ball handler. When his coach substitutes for him during a game near the end of the season, Martin's dad begins cheering for the other team and making disparaging remarks about Martin's replacement. This is done in a relatively quiet gymnasium, with approximately fifty or sixty people in the stands.

Martin hears his father's words and begins to cheer for the opponent also. His coach orders him to stop; he continues; the coach sends him to the locker room.

The father ignores the freshman coach and seeks out the varsity coach after the game. He introduces himself, and addresses the "obvious personality conflict" that exists between his son and the freshman coach, and continues, telling the varsity coach about his own athletic accomplishments and predicting similar feats for his son.

The varsity coach listens and explains that the specific problem must be worked out with the freshman coach, and that he, as head coach, will intervene only if they cannot reach an understanding, which they eventually do, albeit a temporary one.

The following year, the trouble begins again on the JV level. Martin's dad constantly second-guesses the coach aloud in the gym, he shouts instructions to his son that are contrary to those given by the coach, he confronts an opposing player with whom his son has scuffled for the ball, and shouts at him during a timeout, and he abuses officials to the point that one referee comes up into the stands in an attempt to reason with him to quiet down.

The varsity coach observes all of this, and finally, after the game in which the official had entered the stands, he confronts Martin's father, and tells him that he has to change his behavior if he wishes to attend future games.

The father mentions his athletic background and boxing prowess and suggests that they settle their differences "like men." The coach ignores this and continues his attempt to reason. The argument gradually ascends into dialogue, and happily, Martin's father leaves the building that night with a better understanding of athletics within the bigger picture of secondary education, and of the opinion that he and the coach are really not that far apart in their philosophies.

The coach is able to help Martin's father achieve this frame of mind with the following points of view:

—While screaming at the officials is tolerated at thousands of arenas for amateur and professional games, with bands playing and fans screaming, it should never be tolerated at high-school games, especially in a relatively quiet gymnasium in which virtually every word above a whisper is audible to those who are present. Inappropriate remarks become much more personal and insulting when they are not lost in the din of a crowd. Ultimately, such abuse should not be tolerated at any level, for any reason.

—The basketball program (or any sports program) is a high-school extracurricular activity—a part of the student-athlete's education. This is true for both schools in a given contest. Therefore, as inappropriate as taunting the officials is, a parent's taunting an opposing player is unthinkable. What is truly sad is that such parental behavior is decidedly preadolescent, but the preadolescents learn it from adults.

—While there may be exceptions, extraordinarily loud-mouthed, abusive parents inevitably embarrass their children—the very human beings they allegedly, though ignorantly, claim to support. Let the kids be kids. As much as they appreciate parental interest and attendance at events (some student-athletes do not—they feel pressure when Mom and Dad are present), they in no way need to hear loud, abusive verbiage from anyone, especially their own parents.

—Adolescence is a difficult time of discovery and change even in the absence of athletic endeavors. The last thing that a student-athlete needs is to find a parent and the coach in adversarial roles, be the roles real or imagined. Try this question on for size as a sixteen-year-old: *Should I side with my parent, who brought me into the world, who loves, feeds, clothes, shelters, and supports me? Or should I side with my coach, who accepted me on the team, who teaches me to be an athlete and a player, who teaches me punctuality, teamwork, and responsibility, and who ultimately can play me, bench me, or ask me to resign?*

That's a tough choice that no student-athlete should have to think about, let alone make. Unless a coach is definitively wrong—unprofessional behavior or actions that are harmful to the student-athletes—parents should make every effort to avoid, both publicly and privately, this adversarial role. Coaches should do the same. This leads us to the fifth and final point.

—No parent is as objective about the team as is the coach, nor should we expect any parent to be. When it comes down to making cuts, choosing starters, making substitutions, and selecting strategies and tactics, parents must not interfere. In most cases, coaches do not have one of their own children on the team; parents, by definition, do have one or more children on the team. A coach, unless he or she is masochistic, has the best interests of the team in mind—wants the team to do well; the parent, who undoubtedly does have an interest in the team's success, also has strong biological and emotional ties to a particular team member.

It is much easier for a parent to be happy after the team suffers a devastating loss if his or her child turned in an outstanding individual performance, than it is if the child didn't play, or played poorly. The coach, on the other hand, while he or she does celebrate quality individual efforts, must focus on the bigger picture—the team effort.

When a parent is tempted to publicly or privately criticize the coach, at least one question should be brought to mind: "Would the coach deliberately do something that would adversely affect a team with whom he or she spends so much quality time and effort?" Also, trust that there is much more to coaching well than having played some high-school or college sports or watching the professionals regularly on television.

So, parents, yell and scream all you like at the games. Cheer for your child and for your child's teammates. Be enthusiastic. But please don't use the freedom and anonymity of the stands to abuse the coaches, the officials, or the players. Ask yourselves, "What do I want my child to learn from sport?" Then help provide him or her with the proper environment.

"PARENT OR PAL?—THAT IS THE QUESTION"

In elementary school, Jeff had legitimately earned the reputation as a gifted athlete with less-than-earnest work habits. He played two sports very well and looked forward to playing in high school.

The high-school coaches, however, require a one-month conditioning program for all prospective student-athletes, so Jeff decides to forego sports his freshman year. He wants no part of running or strength training.

Jeff's parents, who have never met the coaches at the high school, tell their friends that Jeff did not participate because of a personality conflict with the coaches. Fortunately, Jeff does participate in the conditioning program during his sophomore year. He makes the team and arrives at a preseason scrimmage under the influence of alcohol. He is suspended according to school regulations, enrolled in a counseling program, and eventually, he rejoins the team.

Toward the end of the season, he misses practice before a tournament game because no one woke him up. He serves another mandatory suspension.

Junior year again finds Jeff in the conditioning program, but he fails three courses in each of the first two academic quarters and is ineligible for interscholastic sports. Still, Jeff rarely brings books home from school, and when coaches and teachers demand that he do so, he simply never opens them.

Jeff's parents were proud of his athletic ability and loved to come to the games, but they rarely got the chance to see him play. By the end of his junior year, Jeff's classmates had competed in some fifty contests more than he had.

Jeff smoked, Jeff drank, and Jeff did little or no homework, and though his parents were aware of this, they were ineffective at dealing with it. Jeff's parents wanted him to like them —to be their friend—but to demand homework every night, no more smoking, and no more drinking, would jeopardize the friendship. They failed to see that confronting Jeff and demanding proper behavior from him, which would undoubtedly be uncomfortable, and possibly even traumatic, for all of them in the short run, would inevitably be in his and their best interests over the long haul.

Their willingness to tolerate his inappropriate behavior was definitely one factor, and may have been the primary reason, why he failed to receive an athletic scholarship to college. Sure, he would have resented their demands while he was in high school, but seeing the result—a partial or free ride to college—he would gradually come to understand why they disciplined him, and he would appreciate their demands all the more.

Parents must be parents first and friends second. If a legitimate friendship forms as a natural byproduct of the love and respect shared while the child is young, all the better. Through childhood and adolescence, a friendship in addition to a healthy parent-child relationship is a bonus; a friendship instead of a healthy parent-child relationship is a mistake.

Love your son or daughter—look out for your child's best interests—be a father or a mother; the friendship will evolve from the quality of effort that you offer as a parent.

"WHEN MY BABY SUCCEEDED, WE WERE ALL DOING WELL, BUT WHEN SHE STUMBLED, THE COACH WAS WHY SHE FELL"

Linda makes a just-opened bottle of champagne appear calm. Enthusiasm brightens her eyes in the classroom and in the gym. She is witty, bright, popular, and an average athlete, but she is an above-average worker and competitor. She loves the practices and the games, and everyone—her classmates, teammates, teachers, coaches, and parents—loves her.

By the end of her sophomore year, Linda has earned a B average, a student government appointment, and one JV and one varsity letter. Her parents attend all of her games, supply snacks for the team members, help with transportation when necessary, and thank the coaching staff, both in person and in writing, for their efforts.

One of her coaches sits Linda down before summer vacation begins and congratulates her on all of her academic, athletic, and social accomplishments. The coach encourages her to keep up the good work, but to keep it all in perspective —not to let all of the popularity and success change what made her popular and successful.

Linda is selected as a cocaptain on one of the two varsity sports she plays as a junior, but she also discovers alcohol a little at a time during this third year in high school. Her discovery does not immediately outwardly affect her performance in school, and it goes undetected by her parents, teachers, and coaches.

September finds Linda back for her senior year accompanied by an additional fifteen pounds or so. During the first two months of the school year, she is caught bringing a six-pack of beer to a school function. The student handbook specifically names expulsion as a valid sanction for drug or alcohol use or possession at a school function, but with Linda's positive first three years in mind, the administration meets with her and her parents and works out a counseling and probation solution instead.

The student-athlete guidelines, separate from the student handbook, cite suspension from a team for a first offense concerning drugs or alcohol, and dismissal for any subsequent violation. The head coach sits down with Linda and explains that she cannot repeat her role as cocaptain, and encourages her to put the episode behind her. She understands and agrees with this course of action.

One month later, one half-hour before the season opener, a game at which Linda would be present, but not playing, her father asks to see the coach. Despite the request's bad timing, the coach meets with him but quickly regrets this attempt to be accommodating.

Linda has waited until this morning to tell her parents that she is not a cocaptain on the team. Her father stands now, accusing the coach of overreacting and of being party to multiple punishments (in-school suspension when the violation occurred, probation, mandatory counseling, athletic suspension, and no cocaptain appointment) for a single offense.

He goes on to say that no college will even consider giving Linda a scholarship now, seeing her earn cocaptain status as a junior but not as a senior, and he concludes with personal criticism of the players who have been selected as cocaptains. Three minutes before the game is to begin, Linda's mother attempts the same scenario, but the coach explains that neither the time nor the place is appropriate for her task. In a subsequent meeting with both parents, the following points are emphasized:

—The administration had been lenient in choosing not to enforce the letter of the law—expulsion. In light of Linda's first three years, the counseling and probation decision kept both the individual student's and the school's best interests in mind.

—College scholarships are earned through demonstrated athletic performance and development potential—no coach would ignore a talented, eligible athlete because she was not a cocaptain during her senior year. An unchecked drinking problem would, however, send a coach looking elsewhere.

—Linda and her parents knew the sanctions for alcohol possession—both for the general student body and for student-athletes—they were printed, published, and distributed, and all of the athletes in the school heard them from their coaches. Student-athletes are dealt with both as students and as athletes, whether they are receiving awards or punishments for their behavior. The claims of multiple punishments were unfounded. No one would refuse to accept both academic and athletic awards at graduation were they to be offered.

—If the parents have a problem with the school's treatment of *their own child*, let's hear it. Let's not hear their opinion about *some other child*—Linda's parents had no business complaining about the coach's final selection of cocaptains, especially in the absence of those students and their parents.

—A cocaptain or captain, among other things, should be a leader, an example, and a good citizen, as Linda had been during her first two years. How could her parents expect that Linda, the only student-athlete on the team who had been caught with alcohol, would be named to this position of leadership and example? She should feel fortunate to still have a place on the team.

—Linda had gained some fifteen pounds over the summer, mostly from drinking beer. It was evident in her general appearance and especially in her face. She came home to her parents' home virtually every night. Did they speak with her? Look at her? Kiss her good night? Granted, the change was probably gradual, but it was substantial.

Parents, pay attention to your children; speak with them; look at them; kiss them good night.

"A BREATH OF FRESH AIR"

Paul transferred into the school for the beginning of his sophomore year. Due to transfer-eligibility rules, in the absence of any extraordinary circumstances for the change of schools, he would not be permitted to play any winter sports. His parents attended athletic meetings in the fall, spoke with the athletic director and the coaching staff, and wrote the appropriate letters to the league office, requesting that the rule be waived due to the circumstances surrounding Paul's transfer. This was a standard procedure for parents to follow.

Due to unidentified bureaucratic problems, Paul's case was omitted when the league sent out the written notices that either granted or refused the waiver requests. During this period of waiting, with the enthusiastic support of his parents, Paul attended all of the team's practices, and sat on the bench in street clothes during the games. Although he might not get the chance to play, his parents attended every game, home and away.

When Paul was finally declared eligible, just before the halfway point of the season, his parents were present, and they reacted as if they had won a million dollar lotto prize. They followed up their in-person thanks with a formal letter to the principal, citing the athletic director and the coaches for their help in expediting Paul's case.

They continued their support throughout the season and for the next two years. Paul's parents paid attention to, spent a good deal of time with, and had no qualms about showing their love for, their son. They also had no qualms about disciplining him and providing stricter academic standards than did the athletic department.

Beyond what they brought with them on their son's behalf, they brought three very important factors on behalf of the coaches and the entire athletic program:

- —They were *interested* in their son's education, and they acted on this interest.
- —They were *present* when their son competed, without being centers of attention. This was fun for them, healthy for him (he enjoyed their presence), and great for the team itself.
- —They were *supportive* of their son, the coaches' philosophies and actions, and the school in general. This sup-

port enhanced the value of their presence, and their presence as parents greatly contributed to a much-needed support system for the school community.

In a nutshell, interest, presence, and support, together comprise an ideal approach for the student-athlete's parents to take. Unfortunately, as you read this, fewer and fewer of our elementary-school, high-school, and college student-athletes come from healthy two parent households. The absence of one biological parent, the presence of a step-parent, the competition between separated or divorced parents, or the appearance of a single parent's boyfriend or girlfriend, all have an effect on the experience of childhood or adolescence. These two stages of growth present substantial challenges to young people; when the parents' problems add to these challenges, the child is often the real loser. What is important to remember in *any* family situation that involves a student-athlete is the purpose behind the individual's participation in sport.

It is not a babysitting service; it is not, in most cases, a preparation for a professional sports career; it is not an opportunity for parents to relive or make up for their lost youth; and it should not be a mandatory, involuntary activity. As we said earlier, it should be a voluntary part of the child's education, and it should be both fun and physically beneficial. If additional positive experiences result, be they social, educational, vocational, or personal, all the better. If not, fun and fitness should be enough.

All of this is admittedly much easier to attain if both parents are interested, supportive, and present. All of this is just as, if not more, important if both parents cannot be interested, supportive, and present.

Ask for help. Ask the coaching staff, the guidance counselor, a teacher, another parent—but ask. Someone will help if you're not sure what to do. No one will guarantee success, but someone will help. Your child is worth the temporary insecurity or uneasiness that you might feel when you admit that you need assistance in a particular area. Believe that anyone whom you might ask has just recently asked for help also—coach, counselor, teacher, or friend. No one has all the answers.

The general approach here is really rather simple in the overall scheme of things. Sure, we all disappoint each other, especially those whom we love, from time to time, but all of this comes naturally if we work at loving.

NCAA, NAIA, NJCAA, NSCAA, NCCAA: WHO THEY ARE AND HOW TO FIND OUT WHAT YOU SHOULD KNOW

The National Collegiate Athletic Association (NCAA) is probably the most readily recognizable organization that regulates a prospective student-athlete's experience if he or she plans to attend one of the more than 800 NCAA member schools. The NCAA's high visibility is due, at least in part, to the composition of its membership, which includes most of the large private and state colleges and universities, as well as many smaller institutions. This membership, in turn, tends to attract many of the more talented student-athletes.

The desire to win, at times all-consuming, on the part of some college personnel and alumni, combined with the potential income from television appearances, primarily for the two most popular spectator sports—Division I men's basketball and football—leads to unethical behavior that is directed toward attracting these talented young adults to, and keeping them in, a given institution. While such behavior is by no means limited to the NCAA membership or to these two particular sports, it is at this level, because of the relationships among winning, coaches' job security, pressure from alumni and administrators, and the potential income for the institution from gate receipts, corporate sponsorship, and television appearances, that the worst abuses have occurred. Below, we will take a look at the type of legislation that the NCAA has in place in its attempt to deal with these problems.

Not everyone attends an NCAA member school, however. The National Association of Intercollegiate Athletics (NAIA), completely independent of the NCAA, has a membership of just under 600 four-year colleges and universities. The National Junior College Athletic Association (NJCAA) includes some 550 junior and community (two-year) colleges. Both associations provide national tournaments in specific sports for their respective members. The National Small College Athletics Association (NSCAA) also provides its 37 member schools, who have fewer than 500 males and/or females enrolled, with the opportunity to play in a national tournament, as does the National Christian College Athletic Association (NCCAA), whose 110 members may also belong to another association.

It is prudent for student-athletes and parents to be familiar with the association(s) to which the institutions in which they have an interest belong. At the end of this chapter, after we take a closer look at the NCAA, addresses and phone numbers, accurate as of January 1991, are provided for all of the above associations.

The NCAA regulations generally concern, but are by no means limited to, professional rulings (defining the professional vs. the amateur athlete), financial aid, general principles of intercollegiate eligibility, recruiting rules and regulations, and academic eligibility. It should be noted that NCAA member conferences, such as the Big East, the Atlantic Coast Conference, and the Big Ten, and the individual member schools also have their own constitutions and bylaws that relate to the above concerns.

While student-athletes who are interested in attending an

NCAA member school have undoubtedly heard of NCAA By-law 14.3, also known as "Proposition 48"—the College Fresh-man Eligibility Requirements, a good deal of other informa-tion, both related and unrelated to academic standards is available from the NCAA. Proposition 48 drew much media attention because it most strongly affected the two most tele-vised, most written about, and most income producing sports —Division I men's basketball and football. Other areas are worth knowing about also.

Whether the reader believes that the NCAA is the greatest invention since the wheel, the worst case of unenforceable bureaucratic bungling, or something in between, knowledge of the association's rules and regulations is essential for the college-bound student-athlete, his or her parents, and his or her coach, if an NCAA member school is the intended desti-nation. The risk of an innocent mistake, whether it involves financial aid, academic eligibility, recruiting, or amateur status, is simply not necessary and definitely not worth a year or more of athletic participation. An extreme, but very real, example of the need to know (and, arguably, the inequitable enforcement of the rules at times) appeared in the "Score-card" section of *Sports Illustrated* on September 28, 1987. The piece was entitled "Spiked."

> In recent weeks the NCAA has reduced penalties it previously had imposed on 1) Pitt defensive back Teryl Austin for ac-cepting $2,500 from agent Norby Walters; 2) Auburn quarter-back Jeff Burger for being bailed out of jail by assistant coach Pat Sullivan; and 3) Minnesota quarterback Rickey Foggie for receiving a loan of a plane ticket from assistant coach Larry Beckish. Austin, Burger and Foggie had at first been declared ineligible this season for their infractions, but, upon appeals, Burger had his entire eligibility restored, and Austin and Foggie were given two-game suspensions. The decisions, which were all made by the Eligibility Committee, seemed to indicate a

more lenient—some would say more understanding—attitude on the part of the incoming NCAA executive director, Dick Schultz.

Apparently, though, the right hand of the NCAA does not know what the left hand is doing. Last week a different group, the Academic Requirements Committee, denied an appeal by Iowa State in the case of freshman volleyball player Tracy Graham. Her crime? She took the ACT college entrance exam on a date not approved by the NCAA. Graham, a B+ student at North Scott High School in Eldridge, Iowa, scored far above the NCAA-required minimum for freshman eligibility. But she had taken the ACT in July of '86 because she was competing for her track team in the shot put on a nationally approved testing date in April of that year. The NCAA requires that prospective athletes take the ACT on national testing days so it can better monitor the results.

Graham, a three-time all-state player, had no idea that she was jeopardizing her college eligibility. "We're just sick about this," said her mother, Julie Graham. "We had no idea there would be a problem." When asked to comment, Schultz pointed out that it was the fault of Graham's high school advisers and Iowa State athletic officials, who should have informed her of the NCAA rules.

Bill MacLachlan, the women's volleyball coach at rival Drake University, was outraged. "I guess you have to get bailed out of jail by your coach, accept money from agents or take illegal loans from coaches to be able to get your eligibility back," wrote MacLachlan in a letter to *The Des Moines Register.* "This is a senseless tragedy that leaves me disgusted, mad and wondering *Why?*"

Why? One hesitates to think that it's because Tracy Graham does not play big-time college football. For now, blame it on the inconsistencies inherent in the labyrinthine committee structure of the NCAA.

It is obvious that self-education is a worthwhile avenue to travel. Rules change in any organization as perceptions and needs are altered, so a list of current regulations here might quickly become obsolete, helping no one, and confusing everyone. What I'd like to offer instead are, first, a reference guide to the general areas of concern and the types of rules that are legislated by the NCAA, and second, information—both phone numbers and mailing addresses for the NCAA, the NAIA, the NJCAA, the NSCAA, and the NCCAA.

WHAT FOLLOWS HERE IS MEANT TO BE A GUIDE TO THE TYPE OF RULES THAT EXIST. IT SHOULD BY NO MEANS BE USED AS A PARTIAL OR COMPLETE EDITION OF CURRENT NCAA RULES AND REGULATIONS.

THESE GUIDELINES DO NOT NECESSARILY APPLY EQUALLY TO DIVISION I, II, AND III SCHOOLS.

THESE GUIDELINES APPLY ONLY TO NCAA MEMBER SCHOOLS.

USE THE INFORMATION PROVIDED AT THE END OF THIS CHAPTER IN ORDER TO GET UP-TO-DATE INFORMATION ON RULES AND TO HAVE SPECIFIC QUESTIONS ANSWERED.

WHAT FOLLOWS HERE **IS NOT** A LIST OF RULES, BUT AN OVERVIEW OF THE TYPES OF AREAS REGULATED BY THE NCAA.

Professionalism

Professional athletes, those who are paid for their participation, are generally ineligible to participate in NCAA sanctioned sports. The NCAA does, however, differentiate between athletes who are paid to participate and athletes who are paid to coach or instruct other athletes. Professional status in one sport will not necessarily render an athlete professional in all sports. The rules here are very specific and should be carefully considered by student-athletes who wish to retain their NCAA eligibility.

Financial Aid

Student-athletes can and do receive financial aid based on their athletic ability. The amount and type of such aid is legislated by the NCAA. Generally speaking, the benefits that a student-athlete receives may not exceed those services that are available to the rest of the student population (typically, tuition, room, board, and books).

The NCAA, again, is very specific here, and it is wise for the student-athlete and his or her parent or guardian to acquaint themselves with the rules. Generosity can be a wonderful trait, but only when it is motivated by ethical and legal intentions. See Chapter Ten, "Cheating," for more on this.

General Eligibility

The provisions for general eligibility are concerned with such diverse but basic matters as participation in NCAA-approved high-school all-star games, fraudulent financial reports or academic transcripts, proper admission to school and enrollment in classes, enrollment in a program that leads to a legitimate degree, and athletic eligibility while attending graduate school. High-school coaches should be aware of these regulations, especially those that govern all-star games. Still, self-education is an advisable path to follow for the concerned parent or guardian and the student-athlete.

Recruiting Rules and Regulations

Recruiting guidelines are perhaps the most detailed, and at first glance, the most complex rules offered to the student-athlete and his or her family. Given an unhurried, genuinely interested reading, however, one point at a time, these regulations are both understandable and to the point—whether one agrees with them or not.

Some of the major areas of concern deal with:

—Definition of the "prospective student-athlete": The NCAA defines exactly how and when a high school student-athlete becomes a "prospective student-athlete" who is subject to the association's recruiting rules and regulations. Some of the factors that are considered in determining whether or not an individual is a prospective student-athlete are:

—Has the institution provided transportation for the student-athlete's visits to the campus?

—Has a staff member or representative initiated phone contact with the student-athlete or his or her family or guardian for recruiting purposes?

—Allowable visits to an interested college by a prospective student-athlete: The NCAA is concerned with both the number and the nature of such visits. Several examples of the areas of concern follow:

—Differentiating between "official" and "unofficial" visits.

—How many visits are allowed?

—What may be the duration of the visit?

—What legitimate reimbursements may be made for the student-athlete's expenses?

—Allowable off-campus contacts by a staff member or a representative of a recruiting college: Again, the NCAA is concerned with the number and nature of such contacts. Some examples of their concerns follow:

—Who is a "staff member" or "representative"?

—How many contacts are allowed?

—What may be the nature of the contacts?

—When may the contacts be made?

The NCAA is very specific with regard to who may make these contacts, and when they may be made. Different sports have different periods during which the contacts are allowed.

—Illegal offering of financial aid or other inducement in an attempt to convince the student-athlete to enroll at the institution: The NCAA provides specific lists of what may *not* be done as well as lists of what is appropriate.

—Interested third parties: The recruiting rules are concerned with the behavior of individuals or groups who are outside the college or university and who may make contributions or donations to help with recruitment. The possibilities for such "help" are many and varied, whether it is offered directly to the institution, to the recruit, or to the recruit's family or friends in order to influence the recruit's choice of school. The NCAA prohibits such activity in specific detail.

Again, because of the scope of the recruiting rules, it is essential that student-athletes and their parents contact the NCAA for the association's official publications and to have specific questions answered. What is offered here is an indication of the type of concerns that are addressed. *This is* NOT *a partial or complete listing of NCAA rules.*

The 1990–91 edition of the *NCAA Manual* costs only $11.00. In consideration of the tens of thousands of dollars that a college education costs, the price of the manual seems a modest investment for concerned student-athletes and their families.

Academic Eligibility

This section sets off minimum academic standards that must be met by incoming freshmen or junior college transfers before they may participate on an intercollegiate level at an NCAA member school, and it provides for minimum standards that the student-athlete must maintain in order to remain eligible once such eligibility has been established. Generally speaking, the standards are concerned with such matters as follow:

—The student-athlete's grade point average in the core curriculum in high school: The NCAA specifically defines what constitutes a core curriculum course, and it cites what will be considered its minimally-acceptable grade point average.

—The student-athlete's performance on a college entrance examination—the SAT or the ACT: These standardized tests seemed at first to be a fair measuring tool since they eliminated the inevitable problem with the grade point average—a student with a 3.0 GPA in one school might have extraordinarily different basic skills than a student with the same GPA from another school. Unfortunately, the standardized tests themselves may be biased in fact, if not in intent, against poor, inner-city students. The debate is currently going on, and for good or ill, the SAT and the ACT continue to be used to assess academic eligibility for college-bound student-athletes.

The problem here, however, extends far beyond which measuring tool is used to determine eligibility. The problem extends to the quality of education that is being perpetrated in classrooms from kindergarten through college—a quality that is admittedly excellent for a good many students, but a quality that allows, inexcusably, far too many students to enter high school and even college before they can read and write at an appropriate level of competence. We all have a great deal of work to do in this regard.

The following information will enable you to contact the NCAA, the NAIA, the NJCAA, the NSCAA, and the NCCAA in order to find out what you need to know:

The National Collegiate Athletic Association
6201 College Boulevard
Overland Park, Kansas 66211–2422
(913) 339–1906

The National Association of Intercollegiate Athletics
1221 Baltimore Avenue
Kansas City, Missouri 64105
(816) 842–5050

The National Junior College Athletic Association
P.O. Box 7305
Colorado Springs, Colorado 80933
(719) 590–9788

The National Small College Athletic Association
  1884 College Heights
  New Ulm, Minnesota 56073
  (507) 359-9791

The National Christian College Athletic Association
  P.O. Box 1312
  Marion, Indiana 46953
  (317) 674-8401

EIGHT
Coaching the Student-Athlete

. . . I have admired your work as a coach and your ideal-ism as a man—may both continue and grow in your fu-ture. The greatest thing in the world is the "kids." As long as we profit from their freshness and goodness and give them the benefit of our experience and idealism, there is hope for man's future. Many will seem unappreciative, some will let you down, but, if you love them and you work enough, you will always believe in the next group and in their potential to become good men. I have long believed that I have been enriched by them to a far greater degree than I have been able to enrich them.

THOMAS J. JENSEN, C.F.C.
February 22, 1981

AT A BOYS' VARSITY soccer match between two relatively large schools in the New York metropolitan area, one of the coaches stalked the sidelines in a three-piece suit, with a ciga-rette in hand or mouth throughout most of the contest. His players were often profane toward the officials, and when the match ended in a tie in double-overtime, they accosted the officials, spewing forth more profanity and throwing rolls of tape. The coach either encouraged this behavior or was un-able to control the players, because he did little to halt the abuse. I have erred in my choice of words here; this person was not a coach, but rather a teacher who was supplementing his income. No, he could not have been a teacher either. He was neither a teacher nor a coach—the two are the same— the subject matter differentiates them. This person was a college graduate who was collecting a teacher's salary, which was supplemented by a coaching stipend. He was also a smoker who was not bright enough to understand that there are less-contradictory places to kill yourself than on the sideline during a high school athletic contest—especially when you're collecting the coach's paycheck.

I believe that we should try to avoid such phrases as "The single most important . . ." or "The only thing that matters . . ." I will, however, make an exception to this belief here. In light of such spiritual and worldly events as love, birth, marriage, surgery, war, illness, and death, the single most important characteristic of a good coach is that, win or lose, playing for him or her provides legitimate, ongoing opportunities to become a better human being. Conversely, playing for him or her does not provide any inducement to become a horse's backside.

We must read between the lines here. No one wants brilliant guidance counselors, religious leaders, or psychologists who have no knowledge of sport to coach our young people. Obviously, the athletic and sport-specific knowledge and teaching ability are essential qualifications for a coach. But, as we would not sacrifice these qualifications in favor of the human skills of the counselor, we should not forego the human requirements in favor of some real or imagined, misguided attempts to develop calloused, insensitive warriors, when competitive athletes are what we really want.

Analogies to "battles" and "the enemy" are fine—as long as they are understood as analogies by the athletes. Sport is not war, parallels though there may be. The object of war is to win at all costs, including the cost of killing the opponent. This is not the object in sport—not even in the professional boxing ring, on the football field, or on the hockey ice.

*   *   *

If the members of a particular team behave like goons, or jerks, or bullies on the playing field, in the classroom, or in general, the coach is probably guilty of at least tolerating, if not encouraging, such behavior. Obviously, however, no coach is, or should be, completely responsible for every player's behavior twenty-four hours a day. We don't hold the classroom teacher responsible, or the counselor, or the principal, or the president, or even the parent, so we should not reward the coach in this way either. Yet, the coach's level of tolerance, if what he or she says really means something to the players, can be a strong behavioral force.

At his clinics, Bob Knight teaches coaches what may be the simplest, most basic behavioral tool that a manager of people can use. Whether you are in a classroom, a gymnasium, an office, or your living room, it is valid. Tolerance and satisfaction—the level of behavior or performance that you, as a coach, teacher, manager, or parent, are willing to tolerate is the level that will satisfy your players, students, subordinates, or children.

Demand punctuality, neatness, and respect; enforce your demands fairly and consistently; and acknowledge, with reasonable rewards and sanctions, those who meet and those who fail to meet these demands; and punctual, neat, respectful behavior will satisfy your charges.

Tolerate lateness, sloppiness, and disrespect; and late, sloppy, disrespectful behavior will satisfy them. Sure, there will always be exceptions, but as a general rule, tolerance and satisfaction work. Energy and dedication are essential on the coach's part.

Why do you coach? What is it that you enjoy? Is it a love for a particular sport? The sense of satisfaction in helping a group of individual athletes become a team? Do you like seeing your quotes in the paper? Is it the game situations and decision-making that you like, or do you thrive during the practice sessions?

Are your practices organized? Do you write your practice schedule down? How many minutes of your 90 or 120 do you waste because you are not properly prepared? Unexpected, immediate situations or emergencies are one thing; poor organization is another. How do you deal with tardiness or unexcused absence? Are these transgressions tolerated or are they consistently and fairly discouraged? Do you stand, kneel, or sit down while you put your student-athletes through their paces?

Do you develop your athletes? Is your coaching limited to team concepts, or do you also teach, drill, and develop individual skills? Granted, in some sports this is not a factor—but in team sports, such as basketball, soccer, football, and hockey, both team concepts and individual skills are essential. For example, as a basketball coach:

You are teaching a 1–3–1 half-court trap, so you define the point, wing, middle, and baseline spots; you show the initial set; you demonstrate the correct slides based on ball movement and offensive location; and you're proud once your players understand that the zone will be a 2–2–1 once the trap is set. You've coached the hell out of the 1–3–1 trap, but you've ignored the fundamental defensive skills—proper stance and footwork for each position, how to deny the middle or cut off the baseline, how to trap (where should the trappers' hands and feet be?). All of the lumber and hardware are perfect, but the mechanics don't know how to use the tools—if the building gets built at all, it will be the result of a combination of good raw materials, luck, and natural talent, and not the result of a well-planned and properly organized effort.

Or, you've designed an original offensive system for use against man-to-man defenses, and with several adjustments, it can be used against zones also. You explain it, chalk it, demonstrate it, walk through it, and drill, drill, drill, until the players are making the cuts in the hallway on the way to class. Still, if you don't teach basic dribbling, passing, cutting, screening, and shooting fundamentals, the offense will never work optimally.

The only possible, but still unjustifiable, substitute for proper individual development is superb natural talent. If you allow talent to cover up for your inadequate player development, you cheat the athletes. The gifted athlete deserves as much of a chance to learn the fundamentals as does the below-average plugger. Don't substitute your players' natural abilities for your coaching responsibilities. If you win every year, but your athletes never really improve, you are selling them short. If anything, demand more of those who are capable of doing more.

Teach your golden-armed quarterback exactly how to make the hand-off; your homerun hitting right-fielder how to set up for the throw before making the catch; your lightning-quick point guard how to defend the two-on-one break. Develop your athletes.

What you say should mean something to the student-athletes, so you should say meaningful things. You can be their buddy for life—*after* graduation. If you do not demand a high quality of effort from them, if you do not challenge them, if they do not perceive you as anything more than the person who supervises the practices and the games, you are not doing your job.

Stand for something. Let them see that you really do believe in the values that you try to teach them. As much as what you say *should* mean something to them, what you do *will* mean something to them. Do what you mean to do.

Would you rather coach your team to a well-played, quality-effort loss against a superior opponent, or to a lackadaisical, sloppy, effortless win against an inferior squad? There should be some correlation between your answer to this question and your answer to the earlier question concerning why you coach.

Granted, the win is attractive whether you have a thoroughbred team on its way to an undefeated season, or a marginal group of pluggers whose wins are few and far between. Still, the question has a direct bearing on our understanding of *winning, losing,* and *competing,* and even on the basic concept of the *quality of effort.* While it is healthy for the student-athlete to want to win, and, win or lose, to understand the significance of the quality of effort, it is a virtual moral obligation for a coach, especially a coach of youngsters and young adults, to teach and emphasize the quality of effort as a primary goal in sport.

If the only experience that you as a coach prepare your players for is winning, then your players will be frequently unprepared, unless they are both very talented and very lucky for the rest of their lives. If you prepare them to put forth a high quality of effort in both practice and competition, they will never be unprepared. Remember, the result in the scorebook is relative—the World Champions will always beat the local Little League team, and school A might always defeat school B. The quality of effort, however, is absolute—the World Champs, the Little Leaguers, and schools A and B can all put forth their respective highest quality efforts despite their relative inferiority or superiority and regardless of who finishes with the winning score.

So, if you choose to coach, coach your players and not just your sport. Make sure they have fun, but you don't have to sacrifice fundamentals and responsibility for frivolity. Pay attention to all of your athletes. Don't assume that the talented players know all that they need to know, or that the less-talented kids don't need to know too much because they can't use the knowledge anyway. Pay attention to their academic performance and to their moods. Speak to them about matters other than the team or the sport. Let them know that you are aware of their lives beyond the arena.

NINE

Drugs, Sex, and the Student-Athlete

I HAVE ATTEMPTED to focus on the "what to do's" rather than on the "what not to do's" for the readers of this book. My original outline intentionally omitted any reference to some of the primary pitfalls that hinder the progress of too many student-athletes. As the writing progressed, however, one idea led to another, and I realized that any deliberate attempt to ignore such issues would, at best, leave a large gap, and, at worst, render the book incomplete and myself irresponsible. None of these possibilities is acceptable.

For our purpose here, the word *drug* refers to any substance, natural or man-made, that affects the mind's or the body's ability to function. More specifically, we're concerned with those drugs that have not been prescribed by a physician for a particular medicinal use. These substances include, but are by no means limited to, the likes of alcohol, cocaine, marijuana, crack, heroin, anabolic steroids, and the catch-all categories of pills known as "uppers" and "downers." Though usually considered in a different light because of a historic social acceptance that makes them all the more dangerous, alcohol and nicotine, and to a lesser degree, caffeine, are among the most popular tempters of the young.

All of these substances, in varying degrees, alter the user's heartbeat and/or perception of reality, affect the central nervous system (and therefore the body's ability to function normally), and are either addictive or habit forming. From the mild sense of relaxation that is brought on by nicotine to the strong high of cocaine, all of them, too, either directly or indirectly, have killed people.

The relative degrees of danger and the quickness with which the damage can occur vary from drug to drug. Witness the long-range problems that nicotine from cigarette smoking can do—the short-term calm and relaxation surface years later as cancer, emphysema, heart disease, or complications during pregnancy. Witness then the extreme cases of cocaine use—in 1986, in separate incidents, three healthy, young, elite athletes died quickly when their bodies could not handle the immediate changes brought on by their experiences with cocaine. Those who escape this quick death, if they are "lucky," come to realize that they are killing themselves gradually with their habit instead.

Alcohol, the most consistently popular drug among young people, affects us immediately as a depressant, although boisterous behavior may appear first as the judgment areas of the brain become depressed. If consumed in sufficient quantities, alcohol will impair speech and motor areas, and in sufficiently larger quantities, vital areas can be affected and even shut down, resulting in coma or death. More often though, alcohol provides us with short-term illness in the form of a "hangover," after which, the possibilities that result from continuous, excessive use are extensive and varied—psychological and physical dependency (alcoholism), liver disease, heart disease, unemployment, family abuse or neglect, broken hearts, broken dreams, and death.

The question arises now—why does a student-athlete choose to use drugs? The student-athlete chooses to use drugs for many of the same reasons that anyone does so—to escape the problems of the everyday world; to gain social acceptance; to enjoy the short-term effects of the drug; to overcome boredom, be it real or imagined; to experience the thrill or the challenge of forbidden areas; and in the specific case of the athlete's abuse of anabolic steroids, to find an illegitimate way to increase strength at great risk in order to perform better.

Perhaps the best example to help answer the above question is to consider why so many loving, intelligent, hardworking, family-oriented, and otherwise healthy adults still smoke cigarettes despite the links to cancer, heart disease, lung disease, pregnancy complications, stained teeth, and rancid breath. Surely they do not *want* to develop debilitating or terminal illnesses that would place tremendous burdens on their loved ones. Yet they continue to smoke despite the danger. Why? Beyond the ongoing debate as to whether cigarette smoking is simply a habit or actually an addiction, I believe that three factors contribute to this paradoxical behavior:

—The universal need that *we all have* for immediate gratification—smokers enjoy the act of smoking. It helps them relax.

—The subconscious belief in our own invincibility and immortality—despite a knowledge of and a belief in the dangers, many smokers believe that "it" can't or won't happen to them. After all, there are many people who have smoked for years and who seem none the worse off for it.

—Our inability to delay gratification—directly related to both of the above, is the failure to see the big picture. It is very difficult for many of us to alter our current behavior based on some potential consequence that may be years away. We cannot, or choose not to, forego some short-term enjoyment in order to avoid the prospective negative effects.

The ability to "see the big picture," to choose the most sound, long-range course of action, requires wisdom, and wisdom requires knowledge, experience, understanding, and good judgment, among other qualities. I don't recall feeling particularly wise as an adolescent—invincible, maybe; immortal, at times; but not wise.

The ability to delay gratification is a gradually learned discipline; we do not have it at birth; some of us never learn it. As we experience life, we mature, and we come to understand our personal priorities; we make better decisions concerning our needs and the appropriateness of immediate or delayed gratification. While youth may be "wasted on the young," generally speaking, wisdom is not. We cannot expect the invincible fifteen-year-old to see the big picture, when the panorama regularly escapes even the adult who is two, three, or four times his age. Honest, accurate, continuous education is essential.

The labels on cigarette packs, the horror stories of alcohol- and drug-related deaths and dependency, and the offensive nature of secondary cigarette smoke to nonsmokers and smokers alike, obviously do not deter everyone. So, we must continuously *pay attention* to those we love, our young athletes—anyone at all—to help them understand what is required to choose well.

Sex, between two mature, loving, responsible, and healthy individuals is one of the most pleasurable experiences that two people can share. If any or all of these four adjectives are missing, however, the experience can have an adverse physical, emotional, financial, or even terminal effect on the individuals' lives.

Earlier, I mentioned that it is important that children be allowed their childhood. We don't need fourteen-year-old adults running around, and fourteen-year-olds do need their adolescence in order to become healthy adults. Teenage pregnancy, parenthood, abortion, sexually-transmitted disease, emotional stress and trauma, and AIDS all provide adult-sized problems for individuals with adolescent-sized problem-solving capacities. Any of the above situations, even

healthy, desired pregnancy and parenthood, is a cause of
stress for an adult; adolescence, a stressful time of change
and growth in and of itself, makes such problems all the
more difficult with which to deal.

The day-to-day experiences of adolescents in this country
encourage sexual activity. Advertising presents everything
from clothing to cars to cigarettes by using attractive, and
often provocatively posed and attired models and actors.
Movies without direct or implied sexual activity are rare, and
many television series imply that illicit, extramarital sex
(usually coupled with some type of unethical business deal)
is the accepted, ordinary, and popular way of living. Much of
this is, at worst, a mild annoyance or even a source of amuse-
ment to a healthy, balanced adult; unfortunately, for many
children and adolescents, it is a source of input about the
adult world, and a source of role models, especially when
live, familial role models are missing.

Again, the problem with all of this is that sex, between two
mature, loving, responsible, and healthy individuals, is not
evil—it should be a beautiful, shared experience. Good fic-
tion, or movies that depict true stories, if they are to be hu-
manly accurate, cannot ignore or banish sex. The trouble begins when the viewers, young or old, forget that what
happens on the pages or on the screen is make-believe, between fictional characters or actors and actresses, and that
living out the same scenes in real life can carry some very
serious, and often undesirable, consequences.

We feel the lumps in our throats when the fourteen-year-
old Olympic-hopeful runner gets pregnant and never com-
petes during her last three years of high school. We resent the
fifteen-year-old father, who at first wants nothing to do with a
child, and demands an abortion. We feel our adrenaline kick
in as she convinces him to change his thinking, and together,
they see the birth through and share the parenting. And, finally, we're on our feet with tears in our eyes, when at
twenty-one, she hits the tape first in the Olympic 1500 meter

final, with her husband and seven-year-old child in the stands.

Unfortunately, most teenage pregnancies don't follow that particular, or any vaguely similar, course. Some lead to abortion, which may lead to related physical and emotional problems. Virtually all will involve some level of family and social embarrassment and misunderstanding. All will alter the youngsters' immediate lives—from the classroom experience to extracurricular activities to social events to personal goals. Stress and anxiety will arrive, unpack their bags, and stay well past the abortion or birth. In short, the pregnant child, and not often enough, the responsible father, will have deprived themselves of an important segment of their adolescence.

One other possibility must be considered. Instead of, or in addition to the pregnancy, one of the partners passes along a sexually-transmitted disease, or, in a worst-case scenario, AIDS, to the other. These possibilities are real; they do happen. So, why take the risk? Generally, for the same reasons that people follow any other unnecessary, risky course of action:

—Immediate gratification—sex feels good; it is an immediately enjoyable experience.
—Invincibility and immortality—despite the knowledge of unwanted pregnancy, abortion, and disease, we feel that these things cannot or will not happen to us.
—Inability to delay gratification—we are unable to see the big picture in the heat of the moment. With sexual activity, as with smoking or drug abuse, it is difficult to alter immediate behavior because of some possible future consequence.

Again, education is the key. Understand what the risks are, develop the mind set to avoid them, and believe that sex is all the more pleasurable and relaxed when the partners share this understanding, a more experienced world-view, and most importantly, love that goes beyond a mere act of physical intimacy—and now we're bringing the big picture into focus.

We can't relive our childhood and adolescent years if we miss them by being forced into an adult lifestyle too soon. We can, as adults, however, continue to become better at loving and at making love with each new day of our lives. It makes sense to do these things in the natural, logical order—childhood, adolescence, adulthood—without unnecessary haste.

TEN
Cheating

TOO MANY PEOPLE CHEAT. This does not imply that there is some minimally-acceptable level of cheating. No implications are intended. People cheat. They should not.

Cheating takes on various forms in sport. Athletes, through laziness, can cheat themselves and their teammates. Through performance-enhancing drugs, they cheat their opponents and themselves. In interscholastic and intercollegiate competition, athletes cheat academically in order to earn and maintain eligibility.

If coaches advocate or tolerate grade changes or course selections that will result in below-average grades for a degree that barely amounts to another elementary-school diploma, despite the words "high school" or "college" or "university" thereon, they cheat. The administrators and faculty who allow this behavior also cheat.

Coaches cheat when they violate recruiting guidelines. On a college level, this may entail illegal contact with a prospective student-athlete; it may take the form of an improper inducement—gifts or money or empty promises. When a coach tolerates illegal or inappropriate behavior from an athlete—assault, vandalism, drug involvement, sexual harassment, public nuisance, drunkenness, or what have you—the result is cheating.

The above list is illustrative, not exhaustive. What follows will take a closer look at the specifics and attempt to find a common thread woven throughout this tapestry of fraud and dishonesty.

Lack of Effort

A talented athlete refuses to work at his or her skills and relies on natural gifts in order to get by throughout his or her career. Whether such a career ends on a high-school, college, or professional level is immaterial. The athlete will never know how good he or she may have been—what personal records may have been set—what satisfaction or reward may have been derived—had something more than a minimum effort been made.

In an individual sport, the argument goes, if the athlete chooses to underachieve, and the lack of effort affects no one else, it's the athlete's own business. The right to gauge one's efforts according to personal aspirations is inherent, although it is still a shame to watch natural gifts go to waste. From a coach's standpoint, the obligation exists to demand excellence from this athlete—to encourage a quality effort rather than to tolerate a minimal one. If we look back at the relationship between tolerance and satisfaction, the minimum will satisfy the underachiever if the coach is willing to tolerate it. If a quality effort is never demanded, no one will ever know how this athlete would have responded to such a demand. The coach owes himself and the athlete the opportunity to find out.

With a team sport, the situation changes immediately in that the lack of effort directly affects others. As discussed in Chapter Three, some athletes are gifted to the point that they can defeat many competitors with minimal practice and preparation. If such individuals are not intrinsically motivated to improve, convincing them that such improvement is necessary, or even desirable, may be a monumental task.

More often than not, a young athlete will be motivated by relative results. The concept of personal excellence, with the self as the main focus of competition, must be taught. Why should he worry about improving as long as he can defeat all the kids on his block, or on the team, or in the school? The relative answer is that tomorrow someone better may move to the block or join the team, or the school may compete against an opponent whose every player is a superior athlete. The absolute answer, again, is that the athlete should evaluate his performance according to personal potential, and not according to the performance of others.

At any given point in time, the words "there's always someone better" ring true for all of us. At various stages of their careers, the likes of Kareem Abdul-Jabbar, Mary Slaney, Jack Nicklaus, Muhammad Ali, Edwin Moses, Wayne Gretsky, Larry Bird, Jackie Joyner-Kersee, and Chris Evert, among many others, have earned the title, *best*. If these gifted individuals saw fit to work hard at their respective sports, and they all did (some still do), then the rest of us would be well-advised to do the same—especially when our efforts affect our teammates' chances for success.

Performance Enhancement through Drugs

Performance enhancement and recreation are the two primary motives for drug abuse by athletes. Anabolic steroids are the prominent performance drugs; alcohol and cocaine and its derivatives most often tempt the recreational abuser. Abuse for either reason cheats the athlete, the competition, and, where relevant, the teammates.

An athlete's decision to attempt to improve performance through the use of drugs is directly tied in with Chapter Four's coverage of winning, losing, and competing. For the steroid user, the drugs are either an ill-advised shortcut to a point that would have taken too long (in the athlete's mind) to reach, or they are an inappropriate means to an end that the athlete has no business reaching—a level of strength, size, or performance that is attainable only with the drugs, and one that carries with it a very serious risk to the abuser's physical and emotional health.

In both of the above cases, competition and the quality of effort have been shunned in favor of an unhealthy desire to win at any cost. Again—the desire to win is normal, healthy, admirable—it makes sense to enter any contest prepared and with the intention of winning by honorable means. Once this desire becomes so strong that the nature of the means no longer matters, a problem exists.

The abuser may cheat himself in several ways. While steroids are being used, the participant cannot know his natural performance potential, something that should be of importance to a true athlete. Whether the performance in a particular sport will be measured as a function of speed, strength, appearance, or some sport-specific skill that is enhanced artificially by a drug-induced increase in speed or strength, the result is the same. The sprinter, the weight lifter, the body builder, the football player—whoever uses the drug—must eventually face up to the following:

- —If he is victorious in the particular event, in the game, or throughout the season, he may never know if he could have achieved this victory without cheating (using the drug).
- —Directly related to the above, the victorious steroid user knows that his victory was drug-enhanced, not natural, and essentially, not legitimate. Does this illegitimacy really matter to a cheater? Probably not. Should it matter to an athlete? Definitely so.
- —The physical and emotional problems, some of which may be irreversible, that can result from the use of steroids, simply are not worth the risk for a short-term, illegitimate competitive edge.

Finally, the steroid user cheats the opponent. Even if a victory attained illicitly through a drug-enhanced performance is eventually reversed, and the rightful winner is acknowledged, some irreversible events have occurred.

Track, particularly the sprints, is an excellent example of this. A sprinter wins a race by a tenth of a second with a steroid-enhanced performance. The second place finisher, the rightful winner, crosses the finish line after the tape has been broken, and if there is an awards ceremony, receives the second place prize. Subsequently, after the drug tests have been completed, and the cheating exposed, the abuser is disqualified and the apparent runner-up becomes the winner. This new, rightful winner has been deprived most significantly of the experience of crossing the finish line first, and also of being properly acknowledged at the awards ceremony. This injustice is intolerable whether the race is a high-school dual meet or an Olympic final.

Regardless of the particular sport or event, a steroid-enhanced victory is not a victory at all, but rather, a theft. The thief's booty may include a medal, a ribbon, or a trophy, but it always includes an irreplaceable experience in the life of the opponent—a true athlete.

Recreation through Drugs

Recreational drug abuse also cheats both the abuser and the competition. In Chapter Nine, we addressed some of the possible physiological, emotional, and social effects of alcohol and cocaine. Simply put, from the athlete's standpoint, the drugs diminish the abuser's performance. Unfortunately, some elite amateur and professional athletes are so gifted that even their drug-diminished performances exceed those of many opponents. Like the lazy athlete, however, whose inadequate efforts prevent him from ever realizing his true potential, the recreational drug-abuser will also fall short. He may be good enough to beat an opponent, but he'll never know how good he could have been had he competed without the drugs.

Finally, and this is the one that gets to the heart of competition, a true athlete does not want to compete against an opponent who has a built-in excuse. This does not contradict our earlier contention that our real competition is the self—personal potential. It is. Head-to-head competition is an integral part of most athletic events, however, and as discussed in Chapter Four, an able opponent can push us to greater heights. What is important is that, win or lose, neither of us has an excuse.

Academic Cheating

Young children and adolescents, under the pressure to pass tests or complete homework correctly, a pressure that may be applied by parents, peers, teachers, or the students themselves, sometimes choose to cheat. The cheating may take the form of copying homework (or giving homework to be copied), procuring copies of tests before they are administered, or copying or giving answers or using cheat-notes during an examination.

The desire to "succeed," at least in part, encourages this behavior. The fear of failure also motivates. The true essence of the academic cheating mentality, however, lies elsewhere. The students are rarely, if ever, told or reminded that they are in the classroom to learn, to develop intellectually, emotionally, physically, and socially. Ideally, their intellectual development will enable them to learn to learn, to learn to understand, and to learn to apply what they understand to everyday life. Throughout this process, and, hopefully, supported at home, the affective domain will also be addressed and developed—those often conveniently nebulous concepts of good and bad, right and wrong, truth and deceit.

Unfortunately, too many students, from kindergarten right through graduate school, are conditioned to believe that the report card—doing well with their grades at any cost—is the ultimate goal in school. Who cares if you remember or understand anything—just get good or passing grades and go on to the next step.

Should we be surprised when some coaches and student-athletes, who have been educated in this way, cheat academically in order to do well on their athletic report cards—final scores and won-lost records? Disappointed, yes; surprised, no.

The problems here, on an institutional level, fall into two very broad categories. In the first, coaches, schools, and athletic associations do enforce academic eligibility standards, and some student-athletes cheat in order to meet them. Again, such cheating may take various forms—from copying homework or a classmate's test answers, to paying someone to take a test or write a paper. In the second category, we find coaches, schools, or associations that either have no standards, or that choose to enforce the standards they do have inconsistently, unfairly, or self-servingly, if at all.

The categories share certain characteristics despite their respective operational differences:

—Athletic participation and/or performance is implicitly more important than academic performance or personal integrity.
—This implication actually becomes part of the student-athlete's education. In the first case, he or she learns that one can cheat, play, and still get a diploma. In the second case, the student-athlete learns from example. The coach or the school's or association's administrators demonstrate that it is all right to break the rules for the sake of sports success.
—In both cases, if the student-athlete does eventually receive a diploma, he or she will not have actually earned it. The requirements will not have been met in either the cognitive or the affective domains.

There is one particular cheating mentality, which, though it breaks no written-down rules, may be the most dangerous and disreputable because of its inherent hypocrisy. As an example, let us say that the athletic association to which the school belongs requires that a freshman student-athlete earn at least a 1.6 GPA for the year in order to make satisfactory progress and maintain his or her eligibility for the following season. Let us say further that the requirement does not call for a grade review at the end of the first semester of the freshman year, but only that the cumulative index for the fall and spring semesters must be at least 1.6.

A freshman athlete earns a 1.0 index in the fall semester. For her to keep her eligibility for the first semester of her sophomore year, she must earn a 2.2 in the spring, which, when averaged with the 1.0, will give her the required 1.6 GPA.

If her coach allows her to play during the spring semester of freshman year, the coach is within the stated rules, but the athlete, despite her inevitable endorsement of the coach's decision, is being cheated:

—In all colleges (I hope), a 1.0 index would be considered below average—a letter grade of D—representative of either lack of effort, lack of ability, or both. Simply put, it is unlikely that this individual learned or did much, if anything at all.

—If the athlete is permitted to play in the spring semester, she is being taught that a 1.0 index and whatever effort led up to it are sufficient for her purposes at the college.

—Therefore, sitting the athlete down for the spring semester is the best decision:

—The *experience* of sitting out is a far superior motivation to work academically (if this is all that is needed) than is the *threat* of sitting out.

—A clear message is sent to the athlete that, in reality, and not just in theory, academic effort and progress are more important than athletic eligibility.

—If the coach is genuinely concerned with the athlete's education, he or she will not allow someone with a 1.0 index to compete. By sitting her down, in addition to what is mentioned above, the coach will also teach a good lesson in delaying gratification—first do what is required (and best for you), and then get what you want (in this case, athletic eligibility).

Two other items warrant our attention here. If grades are changed, or if special courses are created or selected so that student-athletes can earn or maintain their eligibility, again, the student-athlete loses out. The grade change is more readily recognized as cheating. The inclusion of courses in a college curriculum that many sixth-graders could easily pass is a more subtle form of deceit. We must realize that the appearance of a title in a college catalogue under the heading "Course Descriptions," or the perpetration of an activity in a classroom within a geographic limitation that is known as a college or university, does not a college-level course make.

Finally, the obvious must be stated. We learn to write in elementary school, but very few of us—even those who show an early inclination toward writing complete sentences and unified paragraphs—eventually make our livings through writing. Likewise, the young, talented athlete cannot count on earning a living by playing the game that he or she loves. Very few ultimately achieve this goal, and, as many real-life examples demonstrate, those skills that enable one to play at or near the top of a given sport do not necessarily prepare him or her to teach, officiate, broadcast, or write about it.

History has shown that this message, regardless of how many times or by whom it is delivered, does little to affect the behavior of many student-athletes who dream of a professional sports career. So, they must be prepared, academically, affectively, socially, and spiritually, for the day when the truth of this message becomes reality. The student-athlete who receives only playing time and/or notoriety from his or her schooling is cheated. Together with parents or guardians, teachers and coaches, he or she must prevent this.

Recruiting Violations

In Chapter Seven, we took a brief look at NCAA recruiting regulations within the context of the association's guidelines for college and college-bound student-athletes. The regulations warrant further attention here. They exist, depending on one's perspective, to protect prospective student-athletes from an endless barrage of phone calls, visits, and other communications from overzealous coaches, or to prevent the more-talented student-athletes from simply being "bought" by the institution that is willing to spend the most money. The theory is that if all the schools play by an agreed-upon set of rules, the student-athlete will choose a school based on what the overall institution has to offer, rather than on who provides the best entertainment, dinner, or transportation arrangements.

Of course, with only some exceptions, many student-athletes will inevitably choose a school based on the athletic program's (or a particular sport's) reputation and success, and/or the overall approach of and image that is presented by the head coach and his or her staff. The problem occurs when the coaches do not have enough confidence in their own or their school's reputation, and they feel that they must offer the prospective student-athlete an additional incentive in order to convince him or her to attend the school. The additional incentive may take any one of many forms: an extra visit beyond what is allowed by the NCAA; actual cash payment to or entertainment for the prospect during a visit; gifts, such as clothing or footwear; aid, in the form of cash, services, or goods, to the prospect's family; or promises of playing time, fame, or success, which, though possible to fulfill, at best can be nothing more than wishful thinking at the time they are made by the coach.

The number and nature of such incentives are limited only by one's imagination and the degree to which a coach feels that he or she must cheat in order to "properly educate" a student-athlete. Whether the coach cheats in order to get an edge on some more-accomplished opponents, or in order to keep up with others who are already cheating, and even if he does this in the name of providing for his loved ones, he is cheating, and he is wrong. That he does this within the context, or under the pretense, of educating young people is all the more upsetting and ironic, since some of these young people will indeed learn—all the wrong things—from the coach's example.

When student-athletes do select a school based on the coaching staff and the athletic department, rather than on academic opportunities and quality, they are left vulnerable and often choose to transfer if the coach leaves. Coaches have as much right to improve their lots in life by changing employers as do other members of the work force, although some, who seem to have made careers of switching schools, should probably rethink their priorities. The commitment between coach and student-athlete must be mutual.

During the recruiting process, student-athletes should ask the head coach if he or she plans to be around for four years, and the coach should answer honestly. Still, regardless of the answer, the student-athlete should be sure to choose the right school, and not just the right coach or athletic program.

The practice of recruiting violations has trickled down into the high-school ranks as overzealous coaches compete for the hearts, minds, and bodies of talented twelve- and thirteen-year-old children. Recruiting should not even exist at this level—the idea of trying to sell (or buy) seventh- and eighth-graders and their parents in order to convince them to attend a particular school because of their athletic ability is shameful. To offer them illegal or inappropriate incentives in exchange for such attendance is obscene.

The approaches vary. A coach at a school in which tuition is charged might offer a tuition reduction or waiver; a coach at a school whose students must live within a specific geographic area might provide a false address or suggest that the child use Uncle Bob's or Grandma Mary's address, if he or she happens to live in the appropriate location.

Regardless of the approach, the cheating will be rationalized. The cheating coach's school has a better academic reputation than the other schools, so the child will benefit; the parents cannot afford the tuition in the private school, but the inner-city public school is a war zone, so the tuition reduction/waiver is in the child's best interests; or the child actually does spend a lot of time at Uncle Bob's or Grandma Mary's house anyway, so it's almost true that he or she lives there.

Any of these or similar rationalizations will effectively initiate the young student-athlete into the adult world of cheating in the name of athletic "success." Whether he or she recognizes it as such at the time it occurs, or if the realization surfaces years later, the lesson will be that coaches and parents (in fairness, let's not forget the administrators who tolerate this behavior) feel that it is all right to break the rules for the sake of sports. Such a lesson must not be endorsed.

Unacceptable Behavior

Finally, coaches cheat when they tolerate inappropriate or illegal behavior on the part of the student-athletes. Unlike the teachers of many classroom subjects, from the first grade through the senior year of college, coaches are, for the most part, blessed with student-athletes who want to play sports. Not everyone in the required English, history, science, or mathematics classes wants to be there; virtually all of the student-athletes at a given practice or game, save the few who are present due to parental or peer pressure, have volunteered—they have *chosen* to show up. This simple truth provides a coach with both an immense responsibility and a wonderful opportunity.

The responsibility is that of every teacher—guiding and

helping other human beings to develop. The opportunity complements this responsibility—this particular group of human beings—these Little Leaguers, high-school athletes, or college scholarship players—all want, in varying degrees, help with their development. Such interest and enthusiasm can create an exceptional learning environment. Despite this, many more coaches are likely to tolerate inappropriate or illegal behavior than are classroom teachers. Winning at all costs, once again, gets in the way.

With very few exceptions, inappropriate behavior in the classroom is confronted and remedied in a timely fashion by even the merely adequate teacher. Too many coaches, however, some of whom have somehow earned the adjective "good" or "superior" (usually based on their ability to win, not necessarily educate), resort only to warnings or slaps on the wrist when their players break training or curfew rules, miss practice, cut class, or are convicted of criminal behavior. The student-athlete misbehaves (whether he is twelve or twenty, "misbehaves" *is* the correct word), little or nothing is done about it, the team continues to win with all members intact, and those involved learn that they can get away with certain things for two reasons: they are members of a sports team; and winning is more important than any behavioral shortcomings that they might have. This is not a good approach for either parents or educators to take.

As is true with the other chapters in this book, the examples here are meant to be representative—by no means are they exhaustive. Cheating takes many forms, from the underweight canoes and kayaks at the regatta, to the timekeeper with the exceptionally slow (or quick) hands during the closely played contest. Regardless of the particular costume that the cheater wears, his actions cut through the very essence of athletic competition and turn that competition into a theft that should not be tolerated at any level, for any reason.

* * *

Ideally, we should avoid cheating, not for fear of being caught, but because cheating is inherently wrong. With many of the complexities we've created for ourselves as we prepare to enter the twenty-first century, it has become acceptable (and convenient) to bemoan all the "gray areas," be they real or imagined, where right and wrong are not so clearly defined as we might wish. Cheating is not a gray area. It is wrong. From the lazy athlete to the drug abuser to the wayward coach and beyond, a common thread is woven throughout this lack of integrity in sport.

In his remarkable book, *The Road Less Traveled*, M. Scott Peck tells us that, "Ultimately there is only the one impediment [to spiritual growth], and that is laziness" (p. 271). He then gets more specific and develops the idea further:

> For laziness takes forms other than that related to the bare number of hours spent on the job or devoted to one's responsibilities to others. A major form that laziness takes is fear. (p. 274)

Dr. Peck goes on to explain that people resist new information and change in their lives due to a fear that has its basis in laziness—a fear of the work they would have to do to accomplish their goal of spiritual growth (p. 274).

Ultimately, it is this same laziness that leads the student-athlete to cheat himself or his teammates with poor work habits, academic misconduct, or drug abuse; likewise, laziness is at the root of a coach's decision to tolerate or perpetrate inappropriate behavior. Both the student-athlete and the coach who cheat have a fear of failure, and they act out their fear through laziness—their pursuit of an illegitimate shortcut to what they perceive to be success. The final prize is all that matters to them; how they get it matters not at all.

*   *   *

When we step outside of the athletic domain and we address the drug crisis, racism, teenage pregnancy, divorce rates, or legal and business ethics, the general conclusion inevitably purports that education, not stricter penalties (for those problems that warrant penalties), is the only legitimate, long-range solution. The term *education* does not necessarily refer to the formal classroom, nor does it preclude that setting, and, like it or not, even if you're tired of hearing it, no one has come up with a better approach.

Cheating is no different: education, especially education by experience and example at a very young age, is the only legitimate remedy. Ideally, such education would not so much remedy, as prevent, the cheating mentality. Will we ever completely eliminate this problem? Probably not, but that is not the immediately significant concern. If enough good people take the time to recognize cheating and draw attention to it, we can render it much less popular and acceptable. Again, too many people cheat. They shouldn't.

ELEVEN
The Student-Athlete
and the Classroom

PERHAPS THE MOST FRUSTRATING truth about education from the perspective of a parent, teacher, or coach, is realizing on occasion how much more interested we are today in the things we were forced to study some years ago, *and,* that our children will undoubtedly live through this same realization in the future.

Perhaps the most frustrating truth about education for some students is realizing that someone, somewhere, some time ago, deemed it necessary that certain things are worth learning, and that you are required to *at least* go through the motions of learning them (attend school) during your childhood and adolescence.

Believe it or not, your parents, teachers, and coaches went through it, and many of them viewed the classroom as you do now. So, why are they putting you through it? Not only for what they learned in the classroom, although the ability to read, write, listen, speak, work with numbers, think originally, solve problems, recognize patterns, or apply theories, etc., etc., etc., will pay off as you grow older, but for what they learned after the safety of the classroom ended. Your formal (classroom) education, with all of its publicly, constantly recognized faults and shortcomings, is a privilege, an opportunity that should be cherished. A mind is a wonderful tool—one whose potential and versatility are truly remarkable. Like an athletic body, however, if it isn't properly developed and regularly trained and used, it will grow lazy, rusty —out of shape—and will not function near its capabilities.

Just as feelings of invincibility and the inability to delay gratification can lead to some negative behavior, they can also preclude us from some worthwhile experiences. It is very easy to protest that school is unsatisfactory—that we would rather be anywhere else than in the classroom. *Teachers* feel this as well as students—on the late October, blue-skied, sixty-degree day, with every autumnal color beckoning from the trees. But the honest people know that a greater good is being perpetrated by staying in the classroom—not forever—but for the allotted period of time.

Inside the classroom, someone is learning to read, or write, or get along—and will be that much better able to appreciate all that beckons outside. There is everything right with developing your mind *and* your body—be a balanced being. You *can* compete, think, love, feel, and be well—and not have to sacrifice one for the other. It just takes some energy.

This chapter is decidedly shorter than any other in the book, not because its message is any less important than those of the preceding chapters, but because its message is that which has been implied throughout *The Quality of Effort*. The book is concerned with an honest approach to athletics—one aspect of our educational and life experience. Let's enjoy it, benefit from it, and keep it in perspective.

TWELVE
The Quality of Effort
—Hindsight

THIS BOOK BEGAN as an article (oft-rejected and never published) in the early weeks of 1987. The experiences and subsequent philosophy that led to the article had their geneses some twenty years before writing them down ever occurred to me. My goal, despite sound advice from some good people, was to complete a manuscript that would be both accessible and beneficial to high-school and college student-athletes, their parents, and coaches. Such a broad target inevitably presents the risk of aiming for too much with one shot and missing virtually everything. This risk, for my purpose here, was worth taking.

Due to a little bit of planning and a lot of luck, each chapter, despite being part of what I believe is a unified whole, can be read independently of the others. Admittedly, I would hope that the book is most effective and beneficial when read from beginning to end in its entirety, but I cannot pretend to know the needs and desires of every person who might be so kind as to pick up a copy and peruse it. Please use this book as it best suits you—I'm happy that you're reading this particular sentence right now—satisfy yourself.

One college student-athlete, who read an early draft of the manuscript told me that he skipped the sections on nutrition, the NCAA guidelines, and athletics and life, because he didn't feel they were immediately relevant to his situation. I understood his point of view, but I did suffer from a bit of an author's bias upon hearing his words. The cake may not be as tasty if you skip a page in the cookbook; *Indiana Jones: The*

Last Crusade is a wonderful movie in and of itself, but it rises to another level if you've already seen *Raiders of the Lost Ark*; any one of *The Canterbury Tales* is a gift to behold, but Chaucer gives us so much more when we read the *General Prologue* and the subsequent individual introductions and prologues. Choose your own example—the whole is often more than the sum of its parts.

Several other readers of early editions of this manuscript complained constructively that it only scratched the surface of certain important topics, and that it omitted certain others entirely. I would be the first to agree that, indeed, complete books should be (and have been) devoted to sports physiology and psychology, coaching, parenting, substance abuse, and other areas that I have addressed within the context of this particular approach to athletics and life. An in-depth look at the effects of substance abuse must include, among other areas of concern, the trials faced by the family of the abuser, and the staggering body count caused by alcohol-induced vehicular homicide; an in-depth study of parenting has to take into account the multitude of factors that parents deal with on a day-to-day (or minute-to-minute) basis beyond their children's athletic experience.

Such in-depth treatments are not my intention here. As I mentioned in the Preface, *The Quality of Effort* does not pretend to be the last word on training, coaching, parenting, or any other individual component that affects the student-athlete's approach to sport; rather, I hope, it will be one of the earlier words that interested persons come across with regard to sport, and I hope it will whet their appetites sufficiently to encourage further reading, participation in clinics and lectures, and, ultimately, a healthy, enjoyable, athletic experience.

Finally, throughout the writing process, images from beyond the athletic domain occupied my consciousness and suggested that I keep my own perspective in perspective: Chinese and Eastern European citizens with a publicly-displayed penchant for democracy; more bloodied, mangled bodies in Central America and the Middle East; freedom, finally, for Nelson Mandela; the remains of a bright, innocent, young black man lying cold on the pavement in Brooklyn; prochoice and prolife activists screaming at each other across police barricades, while both pregnant women and unborn human beings suffer; behavior in government, religion, business, and education necessitating that ethics be taught to those already in positions of leadership; terrorism; homelessness; and the list goes on.

Is a concern with athletics frivolous in light of these images? I think not. Secondary, definitely, but not frivolous. Consistent with the theme of balance that weaves its way throughout these pages, sport has its place in our lives. Ideally, the sense of fair play that results from a positive experience with sport could go a long way toward helping to form a mind set among young people that might prevent them from engaging in unfair or wrongheaded activities while they are young, and predispose them to continue to oppose such unfairness throughout their lives.

Appropriately, such a mind set—one devoted to opposing the bad and promoting the good—requires a significant sense of purpose, self-knowledge, and commitment, all of which may be discovered and developed through sport. Young student-athletes who are involved with individual sports choose to sacrifice some social or employment opportunities in order to focus on athletics and academics; those involved with team sports do likewise and possibly learn to play a specific role for the greater good of the team's success. They make a choice and they commit. I have chosen this topic at this time, not because there are no more-important topics, but because of the very worthwhile role that sport has played, and continues to play, in my life.

Vartan Gregorian, president of Brown University, in a conversation with Bill Moyers in Mr. Moyers's book, *A World of Ideas* (originally a series for public television), addressed these concepts of purpose, self-knowledge, and commitment. Their general conversation concerned our changing American values; this particular passage focused on moral commitments, and is, I believe, as relevant within the limited scope of our relationship with sport, as it is throughout the larger scope of American life:

> Total commitment to every good cause is equal to total apathy because you cannot act upon all of them. You have to structure your commitments: first commitment, second commitment, third commitment, fourth commitment, and so forth. You have to structure a hierarchy of commitments. And that's very hard because it makes you think back to the self, to think, what are your value systems? What are your obligations as a human being? What are your obligations as an American? (p. 187)

Thank you, Dr. Gregorian. And thank you, reader, whoever you are. I hope the reading has been as worthwhile for you as the writing has been for me.

Index

Abdul-Jabbar, Kareem, 91
Academics *see* Education
ACT exam, 68
Advertising, 85
Aerobic training, 16-17, 18
AIDS, 84
Alagia, Frank, 10
Albert, Marv, 5
Alcohol, 82, 84
Ali, Muhammad, 91
Anabolic steroids, 82-83, 91-93
Anaerobic training, 16-17, 18
Anderson, Bob, 20
Anderson, Jean, 20
Athletics
    and cheating, 89-103

competition, 33-39
and life, 47-51
practice, 17, 25-31
professional, 38, 69
training, 15-20
see also Student-athlete
Austin, Teryl, 67

Background training, 20
Baker, Charlie, 12
Barnett, Dick, 5
Basilian, Brother, 4
Basketball, 3-13, 18, 38
    see also Jump shot
Beckish, Larry, 67
Bird, Larry, 91
Bradley, Bill, 5

Bullock, Shawn, 12
Burger, Jeff, 67
Byrd, Sam, 12

Calories, 23
Carnesecca, Lou, 12
Catholic High Schools
　Athletic Association, 12
Cheating, 89-103
Cigarettes, 82-84
"Clyde", 5
Coaching
　and cheating, 89, 98-101
　and recruiting
　violations, 98-100
　of student-athlete, 75-80
　and unacceptable
　behavior, 100-101
　see also specific coaches
Cocaine, 82
Commitment, 110
Competition, 33-39, 80, 91,
　93
Conditioning, 15, 16, 18-19
Coordination, 17

Dairy, 22, 23
Dean, Dizzy, 36
DeBusschere, Dave, 5
Delayed gratification, 83-84
The Des Moines Register, 68
Diet, 21-23
Discipline, 50
Dobbs Ferry High School, 3

Drake University, 68
Dronzek, Kenny, 12
Drugs
　performance
　enhancement and, 91-93
　recreation through, 93-
　94
　and student-athlete, 81-
　84

Education
　academic cheating, 94-
　97, 103
　and NCAA rules, 67-68,
　72-73
　quality of, 73
　sport as, 38-39
　and student-athlete, 105-
　106
Effort
　lack of, 90-91
　quality of, 1-13, 80, 107-
　110
Esquire, 36
Evert, Chris, 35, 91
Exercise, 19-20

Fairness see Justice
Fast twitch fibers, 17-18
Financial aid, 69-70
Fitness tests, 3
Flexibility, 19-20
Foggie, Rickey, 67

Food groups, 22-23
Fordham University, 12
Frazier, Walt, 5
Fruit, 22, 23
Fundamentals, 3

Golf, 15
Graham, Julie, 68
Graham, Tracy, 68
Grains, 22, 23
Gregorian, Vartan, 109
Gretsky, Wayne, 45, 91

Hoffman, Marshall, 16, 17,
    19, 20
Houston, Jerry, 5-6, 8, 9, 11,
    12

Ignorance, 53
Injury prevention/
    treatment, 16
Iowa State, 68

Jackson, Phil, 5
Jensen, Thomas J., 75
Jordan, Michael, 45
Joyner-Kersee, Jackie, 45, 91
Jump shot, 27-32
Justice, 1, 41-46

Kelly, Don, 12
King, Martin Luther, Jr., 2
Kingdom, Roger, 36
Knight, Bob, 77
Koch, "K.J.", 12

LaSalle Academy, 5
Laziness, 102
Leonard, George, 36
Losing, 1, 35-36, 80

MacLachlan, Bill, 68
Marra, Don, 3
Mastery, 36
Mattingly, Don, 45
McGugins, Ron, 10
Meat, 22, 23
Mechanical correctness, 25-
    26
Micro-injuries, 19
Milk, 22
Mirkin, Gabe, 16, 17, 20
Montana, Joe, 36
Moses, Edwin, 45, 91
Motivation, 36
Movies, 85
Moyers, Bill, 110
Mueller, Mike, 12
Muscles, 16-20

NAIA see National
    Association of
    Intercollegiate Athletics

National Association of
Intercollegiate Athletics
(NAIA), 66, 73
National Christian College
Athletic Association
(NCCAA), 66, 74
National Collegiate Athletic
Association (NCAA), 65-73,
98
National Dairy Council, 22,
23
National Junior College
Athletic Association
(NJCAA), 66, 73
National Small College
Athletic Association
(NSCAA), 66, 74
Nazareth High School, 13
NCAA *see* National
Collegiate Athletic
Assocation
NCCAA *see* National
Christian College Athletic
Association
New York City Catholic
High Schools Athletic
Association, 12
Nicklaus, Jack, 91
Nicotine, 82
NJCAA *see* National Junior
College Athletic
Association
NSCAA *see* National Small
College Athletic
Association
Nutrition, 21-23

Opportunity cost, 44
Ostrander, Mike, 12
Overtraining, 20
Oxygen, 16

Parenting, of student-athlete,
53-65
Peak period training, 20
Peck, M. Scott, 44, 102
Penders, Tom, 12
Perceived specialization, 48-
49
Performance enhancement,
and drugs, 91-93
Physical fitness, 15-16
Physical well-being, 47-48
Pitino, Rick, 30
Practice, 17, 25-31
Pregnancy, 84-86
Professional athletics, 38, 69
Proposition 48 (NCAA), 67

Quality of effort, 1-13, 80,
107-110

Recruiting guidelines, 70-72,
89
Recruiting violations, 98-100
Reed, Willis, 5
Regulations, NCAA, 66-70,
98
Repetition, 25-26

The Road Less Traveled, 44, 102
Rockland County, 12
Rocky, 48
Russell, Cazzie, 5

St. John's University, 5, 10, 11, 12
Samuelson, Joan Benoit, 2
Satisfaction, 1-2
Schultz, Dick, 68
Serendipity, 44
Sex, 84-86
Sit-ups, 3, 7
Slaney, Mary, 91
Slow twitch fibers, 17-18
Smith, "Beaver", 10
Smoking, 82-83
Southmayd, William, 16, 19
Specialization, perceived, 48-49
Speed, 17-18, 26
Sports *see* Athletics; specific sports
Sports Health: The Complete Book of Athletic Injuries, 16, 19
Sports Illustrated, 67
The Sportsmedicine Book, 16, 17, 20
Stamina, 19
State University of New York at Albany, 10
Steroids, 82-83, 91-93

Strength conditioning, 18-19
Stretching, 19-20
Stretching, 20
Student-athlete
    coaching, 75-80
    and drugs, 81-84
    and education, 105-106
    and NCAA, 65-73
    parenting, 53-65
    and sex, 84-86
Success, 1, 41-46
Sullivan, Pat, 67

Talent, 1, 4, 79
Teen pregnancy, 84-86
Tepikian, Paul, 4
Track, 4, 92-93
Training *see* Athletics, training; Overtraining
Tryouts, 7, 37-38

Unacceptable behavior, 100-101

Vegetables, 22, 23

Waitz, Grete, 2
Walters, Norby, 67
Winning, 1, 33-35, 80, 91-92
Winters, Brian, 27
A World of Ideas, 110

About the Author

REGGIE MARRA COACHED basketball for thirteen years in the New York Catholic High Schools Athletic Association at Sacred Heart High School. He taught in the English, Business, and Religion departments for seven-and-a-half years, and served as athletic director for three years. He has a B.S. degree in Marketing and an M.A. degree in English.

He ran a sub-five-minute mile for the first time when he was thirty-one, and besides running, writing, teaching, and coaching, he enjoys most things that make him sweat, think, or laugh. He dislikes liars, cheats, and bullies.

To anyone who knows him well, he apologizes for not writing a funny book. Perhaps, if enough people buy this one, he'll be able to write a funny one somewhere down the road. Perhaps.

The author and publisher are interested in hearing the opinions, positive or negative, that readers may have on *The Quality of Effort*. Please send your comments to the address listed below. If you include a sentence granting permission, we may use your opinion in future advertising. Thank you for your interest.

FROM THE HEART PRESS
Box 256, Dept. OP
Wykagyl Station
New Rochelle, NY 10804